SUFFOLK
REMEMBERED

Via Ypres (*A record of the Field Ambulances,
39 Div. B.E.F.*)
Suffolk Yesterdays (Reprinted at request of
the London & Home Counties Branch of the
Library Association 1968)
This Suffolk
North-east Suffolk
An Hour-Glass on the Run
A Window in Suffolk
Under a Suffolk Sky
A Suffolk Calendar
In Suffolk Borders
The Felixstowe Story

SUFFOLK REMEMBERED

ALLAN JOBSON

ILLUSTRATED

ROBERT HALE · LONDON

© *Allan Jobson 1969*
First published in Great Britain 1969

SBN 7091 1119 3

.

Robert Hale & Company
63 Old Brompton Road
London, S.W.7

PRINTED IN GREAT BRITAIN
BY EBENEZER BAYLIS AND SON, LTD.
THE TRINITY PRESS, WORCESTER, AND LONDON

To the Suffolk of my Childhood

CONTENTS

ILLUSTRATIONS

FOREWORD

····⚓····

One of the most enheartening pieces of news in this age of spoliation is that the Suffolk coastline and heaths are to be protected, because of their outstanding beauty. This is to come about under the kindly offices of the National Parks and Access to the Countryside Act of 1949, through the Countryside Commission.

The effect of designation is that the Commission is empowered to make grants to the local authorities for various works to preserve or improve the area. Grants could cover the improvement of derelict land. They could also be used for the removal of unsightly buildings, tree preservation and planting and the acquisition of land for public access.

All but the Country Landowners' Association and the National Farmers' Union welcomed the proposal. The two dissidents feared that this designation would lead to a greater influx of sightseers, and thus help to destroy the amenities that were hoped to be preserved. However, after consideration they have withdrawn their opposition.

Such places as the parish of East Bergholt, home of our great Constable; parts of Beccles, where Nelson's parents were married; and Woodbridge, where that kindly and lovely soul, Edward FitzGerald, had a lodgement (including, it is to be hoped, the old Tide Mill); are to be designated conservation areas because of special architectural or historical interests.

It is further added that in these areas extra safeguards will be employed to ensure that development will enhance rather than detract from the local character.

Any excuse, therefore, for yet another book on Old Suffolk

and the South Folk of yesteryear, would appear to be unnecessary. If the past can remain inviolate, we need not fear the future with all its horrifying possibilities but rejoice with Keats in:

A shielded scutcheon blush'd with blood of queens and kings.

A COUNTRY LIFE

Come Sons of Summer, by whose toile,
We are the Lords of Wine and Oile:
By whose tough labours, and rough hands,
We rip up first, then reap our lands.
Crown'd with the eares of corne, now come,
And, to the Pipe, sing Harvest home.
Come forth, my Lord, and see the Cart
Drest up with all the Country Art.
See, here a *Maukin*, there a sheet,
As spotless pure, as it is sweet:
The Horses, Mares, and frisking Fillies,
(Clad, all, in Linnen, white as Lillies.)
The Harvest Swaines, and Wenches bound
For joy, to see the *Hock-cart* crown'd.
About the Cart, heare, how the Rout
Of Rurall Younglings raise the shout;
Pressing before, some coming after,
Those with a shout, and these with laughter.
Some blesse the Cart; some kisse the sheaves;
Some prank them up with Oaken leaves:
Some crosse the Fill-horse; some with great
Devotion, stroak the home-borne wheat:
While other Rusticks, lesse attent
To Prayers, then to Merryment,
Run after with their breeches rent.
Well, on, brave boyes, to your Lords Hearth,
Glitt'ring with fire; where, for your mirth,
Ye shall see first the large and cheefe
Foundation of your Feast, Fat Beefe:
With Upper Stories, Mutton, Veale
And Bacon, (which makes full the meale)

With sev'rall dishes standing by,
As here a Custard, there a Pie,
And here all tempting Frumentie.
And for to make the merry cheere,
If smirking Wine by wanting here,
There's that, which drowns all care, stout Beere;
Which freely drink to your Lords health,
Then to the Plough, (the Common-wealth)
Next to your Flailes, your Fanes, your Fatts;
Then to the Maids with Wheaten Hats:
To the rough Sickle, and crookt Sythe,
Drink frollick boyes, till al be blythe.
Feed, and grow fat; and as ye eat,
Be mindfull, that the lab'ring Neat
(As you) may have their fill of meat.
And know, besides, ye must revoke
The patient Oxe unto the Yoke,
And all goe back unto the Plough
And Harrow, (though they'r hang'd up now).
And, you must know, your Lords word's true,
Feed him ye must, whose food fils you.
And that this pleasure is like raine,
Not sent ye for to drowne your paine,
But for to make it spring againe.

                                 Robert Herrick

BACKGROUND TO LIFE

·◦✠◦·

Ne'r to be found againe.

It is difficult for us now to look back on village life of a century ago without a sense of wonder and nostalgia. Wonder at the mode of life, its simplicity, hardships, thriftiness and fears, coupled with a nostalgia for perfect peacefulness, time to linger, serenity, and even a continuity that have been lost for ever. Not for them wars and rumours of war. Their backward look did not travel further than Trafalgar and Waterloo, battles that had been fought and won, providing them with a security to add to peacefulness; and when the muffled peal was rung for the old Duke of Wellington, they were thankful for his victories. As for Nelson, why he was but a product of one of their rectories. After all, the Doughty family were alleged to have been parsons at Martlesham since the Devil was an infant. Life for them was fixed and continuous, as expressed by the son of yet another, adjacent rectory:

> But what did ye saay, and what did ye do,
> Wi' the butterflies out, and the swallows at plaay,
> An' the midders all mow'd, an' the sky sa blue?
> Why, coom then, owd feller, I'll tell it ta you;
> For me an' my Sally we swer'd to be true,
> To be true to each other, let 'appen what maay
>   Till the end of the daay
>   And the last load hoam.

Or as the old cleric noted it:

> This morning I have put a Tye
> No man could put it faster
> 'Tween Mathew Dodd, the man of God,
> And modest Nellie Foster.
> > John Lewis, Clk.

As we turn those old pages, yellow maybe, they are perfumed with cottage gardens, farmyard manure, beanfields, wallflowers, lavender and thyme; while the daffodils sounded the requiem:

> Faire Daffadills, we weep to see
> > You haste away so soone:
> As yet the early-rising Sun
> > Has not attain'd his Noone.
> > > Stay, stay,
> Until the hasting day
> > > Has run
> But to the Even-song;
> And, having pray'd together, we
> > Will goe with you along.
>
> We have short time to stay, as you,
> > We have as short a Spring;
> As quick a growth to meet Decay,
> > As you, or any thing.
> > > We die,
> As your hours doe, and drie
> > > Away,
> Like to the Summers raine;
> Or as the pearles of Morning's dew
> > Ne'r to be found againe.

Their fields were their horizon, and the distant scene was fringed with trees, enough for them of space and infinity. Their sky was the noblest of mantles, discovered by a miller's son and caught for all time; limned also by that other local artist-poet, John Crome. That was enough. If they lived miles from anywhere they were not lonely; there was so much to see and do about them:

> A hen
> I keep, which creeking day by day
> > Tells when
> She goes her long white eggs to lay.

Of course all was not peace; there were squabbles, more often than not, on the subject of tithes. There was always someone, although he would be a tenant farmer, trying to do the parson out of an armful of this or that or one of his men out of a few coppers. Generally speaking, however, the parson saw to it he got his portion, and even demanded his tithe of sheep to be made at the shearing, not at lambing tide. Yet when he made his record for the year, the most important events for himself and the village would be:

> The paving of ye Chancel
> Setting 6 Apple trees Tumps in ye Dove court Close
> A Quince-tree & some apple trees ith orchard
> Asps in ye Court and stackyard

And, be it noted, he got as much as forty-five shillings annually for pigeon manure. Those destructive warmints that preyed on other folks' fields.

They were wonderfully quick to observe the times and seasons; these governed life, as the entry in the Baptismal Register at Brundish for 1600 shows. "The 26th., daie of October was Baptised Thomas Colbye the sonne of Thomas Colbye, gent, and Annye ux' beinge borne the 13th., daie of October the signe beinge in Taurus at the hower of 7 of the clock in the evening."

The bird of omen for them was the magpie, why I cannot tell. Old women before setting out would take a careful glance as to whether any of these 'owd buds' were about. If there was only one, she would wait until that had cleared off, because:

> One's a sign of bad luck,
> Two's a sign o' good,
> Three's a sign o' a berrin' (or brocken leg),
> An' four's the sign o' a weddin'.

Even children going to school might note the direction of the bird's flight and be concerned as to whether it crossed their path. They would even point a finger to suggest the way it should fly, then make the sign of the Cross with the toe of their boot and spit on the ground.

> I cross one magpie
> An' one magpie cross me,
> May the Devil take th' magpie,
> An' God take me.

But it must have been the children who sang:

> One for sorrow
> Two for mirth
> Three for a weddin'
> Four for a birth.
> Five for a Parson
> Six for a clerk,
> Seven for a babe
> Buried in th' dark.

Or:

> Five for England
> Six for France
> Seven for a Fiddler
> Eight for a Dance.

Old customs still survived, because change came slowly, and they had their little festivals which they so greatly enjoyed. The old term of 'shoeing the colt', was a literate act, and provided a red-letter day at the forge. When a colt came in to be shod for the first time, much to its alarm and annoyance, it was curious how many managed to hear of the event and gather round. When the job was done they would all toddle over to the ancient pub and 'wet the shoes', commenting meanwhile, "Ah hoop t' hoss 'ill make a good un an' grow into money." They knew a hoss when they saw one.

The forge too was a place for gossip amongst the old 'uns, as the pump was for the women. The coachman might come from the Hall and drop a note or two as to who was 'up there'; but he was rather circumspect, being a man a bit up in the world. Then *sotto voce*, "Did yew tewgether hare them shots in the night? Reckon owd Keeper Cady mus' ha' bin asleep, or suffen."

Their speech was golden, as this recorded in a small volume of Norfolk tales:

He saay t' me, he saay, "Whatever arr yew a do'en with that there muck!"

"Aarn't I a loden on it," I saay, "on t'r this here caart?"

"Caart," he saay. "Wor aar yew a go'en' t'r dew with it," he saay "when your ha' loded it?"

"Dew wi' it!" I saay. "Arrn't I a go'en' to caart it inter the garden and spreed it?" I saay.

"Spreed it!" he saay. "I'll *spreed* yew!"

What a lovely bit of conversation to have heard through the hedge, by a wanderer returned to his native!

How oft I've sighted alterations made;
To see the woodman's cruel axe employed,
A tree beheaded, or a bush destroyed;
Nay e'en a post, old standard, or a stone
Mossed o'er by Age, or branded as her own,
Would in my mind a strong attachment gain,
A fond desire that there they might remain.

A SUFFOLK BACKWATER

·····•⟨⬦⟩•·····

"Sorry I won't be able to come and do for a few days," wrote a *Surrey char to her employer, "but my throat has gone again. But I've got my chest back and the doctor says he thinks I'll soon find my legs."*

My mother was born in a most romantic part of Suffolk. Romantic because it was so near the coast and because of the many influences which had come thereby. It is not everywhere that has as a near neighbour a buried capital city, swallowed up by the sea, and it is not everywhere that has seen so much of glory and enlightenment in religious houses, and all the beneficial influences which came through them in hospitals, schools, culture and learning. How splendid it all must have been when the East Anglian kings lived in their palaces and wore that exquisite jewellery that has but lately been unearthed. The palaces may have been only of wood, but they told of a great refinement and of splendid artistry.

Some of the great names of England were connected with these quiet fields, such as the one-time chief landowner, Roger Bygod, Earl of Norfolk; and it was a great Suffolk man, Sir Ranulff de Glanvill, who built and endowed some of its local religious buildings, such as Leiston Abbey and Butley Priory. That was before he died on Crusade under Coeur de Lion at Acre. I cannot do better in this instance than quote from Robert Reyce's Breviary of Suffolk, modernizing the spelling:

When I come to Suffolk Gentlemen to whose beginning, the memory of man alloweth not the contrary, whether of learning, valour, virtue, or any other just cause whatsoever arisen, I find

the number as great as any other places, or shires; yet when I regard the small bounds which this country affordeth, with the
number of Gentlemen therein contained (I mean such as are
Gentlemen of Ancestry) and endued with large livelihoods,
Patronies, and ample revenues, I suppose I should not incur
matter of reproof, if I should prefer this country to many other
shires far greater in this realm. If as many do affirm nobility is
best continued by those convenient means by which at first it did
arise, then no doubt, but the learning, wisdom, heroical valour,
upright justice, approved government, with many other things the
true sources of generosity, all which seasoned and as it were
crowned with the purity of true religion, and godly life, which is
here entertained and embraced among this sort, is the only and
principal cause, why so many worthy families have so long time
remained within so narrow a precinct.

Having swallowed that lot and understood its implications,
remembering too that my mother was born into an Elizabethan
Suffolk only once removed, you would begin to realize how
such an influence surrounded even a poor Suffolk girl when she
set out in life. Fancy taking that sort of background into a little
Victorian house about twelve feet wide and a bit deeper, built
of suburban bricks that had been but newly spilt into a Surrey
field, and where life was lived below the pavement level. True,
she got to like that sort of thing, but she never forgot she was a
Suffolk 'mawther', or the early days that had fashioned her
character and enabled her to hold her head high.

My mother was born in a little cottage, long since gone up in
flames, on what was known as the turnpike. It led from Yoxford
to Leiston, passing through the lovely village of Theberton, and
in early days had been known as Meadow Lane. Even her first
home was steeped in antiquity, for it was at Hog Corner, hard
by Valley Farm, and abutted on to the Packway. This last name
is suggestive and something quite out of this world. That old
Packway, its name unchanged, worn deep by the traffic of
countless generations, led from Dunwich, the city of pilgrimages
to Colchester; at least that is what they said. In those days it led
to Packway Farm and then got lost in a field; but obviously that
had not been its end. In the other direction it passed the stackyard and barns of the Valley Farm by means of a sunken road
known as the Wash, and could be traced back to Rackford

Farm and skirted the village of Westleton by an ancient path, known as Black Slough. These names will at once suggest to you a very early England, peopled by Saxons.

Along the turnpike leading to Theberton, was a tree hidden in the hedge. That was a landmark and a boundary, Yew Tree Corner. Once upon a time a cottage stood there, belonging to the Hall Farm, but it was burned down in 1849. As far as my mother and grandmother were concerned it meant a right-of-way into what was then called Theberton Lawn, and masses of cowslips. These provided the famous country wine, but were also good if you couldn't sleep:

> For want of rest
> Lettuce and cowslip; *probatum est.*

Now when my mother and her sister Rebecca (Bec or Becca for short) went for a walk, they might have gone past Yew Tree Corner and would have come out at the scene of our picture (facing page 33); and I'll tell you why. They had an Aunt Danbrook living at Eastbridge, a mournful place but full of character, and they might have called on her just to give her a treat. How thoughtful of them. She would have been right glad to see them, given them a glass of her cowslip wine, and, if it was a baking day, a rusk just out of the brick oven, with a lump of her country butter. That was all part and parcel of life in those days and taken for granted. But what I want to tell you is that Doughty's *Chronicles of Theberton*, has this: "In 1739 a man named Danbrook was paid for one fox, seven polecats and one weasel." So you see the Danbrooks had been there a mighty long time.

The approach by these two sisters would have been past the lovely tree-sheltered bit of parkland that surrounded the Hall, down a slight dip and then up a gentle slope into the village. And it was that portion of rising ground that provided the picture. It would be difficult to find a more beautiful grouping and setting amid Suffolk oaks. What is more, it must have been very much the same in my mother's young days, as when the photograph was taken. It is an essentially English scene, out of Suffolk, neither Flemish nor Dutch, breathing peace free from restlessness. Although to me, I must confess, it is rather French, reminiscent of Corot.

Here too, in one small spot, the ages blend into perfect harmony, because that lovely old church tower was advanced in years when those cottages were built, when that illustrious princess, Elizabeth, came to the throne. The steep pitch of those roofs suggest they were thatched like the church, and the dormer windows (lucum in old Suffolk) not only add to the symmetry but give light to little sweet-smelling bedrooms and their quilted coverlets. The tiny slatted fence and the children at play add life and laughter to a pastoral scene. Those cottages would have been part of the Church Farm, although the one at this end seems to have got all the chimney.

But it is the church tower that provides the link. The octagon top is much later than the circular shaft, for, whereas the latter is Norman, even pre-Norman, the former is fourteenth or fifteenth century. Moreover, that church, with a parsonage and glebe, is mentioned in Domesday.

Now mother and her sister had to go round by the church to get to Aunt Danbrook's. They could have gone in by a little wicket gate at the end of the cottages and through the churchyard. But in all probability they would have avoided this path as the ancient graves seem a bit piled up, and they might have been scared lest one of the occupants should jump out on them. Whether you liked it or not, Theberton was a rare place for ghosts, with the abbey ruins in Leiston, where you might meet a shrouded figure at any time. It might have been one of the canons, John Yoxford or William Woodbridge. Then the Round House, which was at that end of the Packway, where it got lost, was definitely haunted as everyone knew. They would therefore keep to the road, turn sharp left and follow the lane until they came to that old smugglers' retreat known as the Eel's Foot. In so doing they would have crossed the narrow seas and gone from a Suffolk England into a Flemish Suffolk, with sundry waterways finding a course to the sea. As they skipped along, for they would not have been very old, they might have discussed the merits of the old bells that rang from that Theberton steeple, and their own Middleton bells, but they would not have confused the two.

They would have been poking into the hedgerows, like all country children, to see what they could find in the way of a blossom to take home. They did know of a bank where the dog violet grew, and, although it had no perfume, grandmother dearly loved a bunch, because of its delicate shade of blue. It fair helped to drive the winter away. Then in the distance seaward, but a long way off, might come a dull but clear report. "D'yer hear that Bec?" the elder sister would remark.

"Yes, I do, Liza', that's Aldeburgh way. [It was actually Landguard Fort.] And as long as that don't get any nearer, I 'ont mind! What they want to keep on a wasting them things for, I don't know. After all, old Boney was settled when father was a bit of a boy."

"I suppose they must keep on a practising," replied Liza, "but I hope that 'ont come in our time." She little knew that it was to come in her time, that she was to experience the uncertain horrors of the first; while Bec was to know something of both World Wars, and to be rendered homeless in the second.

Theberton to them was quite different from their own village of Middleton. For example, there was a fen reeve there, and Aunt Danbrook used peat for her fires, dug from the Theberton Bogs and the Common Fen. Then there was a bit of a field known as Hangman's Acre, to be avoided at all costs. The people's names were different—Rouse, Lumpkin, Ford, Todd, Canham, Brown, Free, Mayhew, Marjoram, Shepherd, Foulsham, Newson, Leggit, Broom, Watling and Bidwell. True, you could find some of these in Middleton, but not all. Grandmother was a Brown, but we had better not enquire too deeply into that family, because in 1606 Agnes, the wife of John Browne, son or grandson of Robert Browne, landowner at Leiston and Theberton, murdered her husband at Theberton.

Aunt Danbrook was a widow, her husband, who had been a half-and-halfer (that is a part-time fisherman) was drowned at sea. She lived in a little low cottage within sound of the waters that had engulfed him. On the roof was a fine specimen of a houseleek which always intrigued the girls because it never failed even if it was a hot old summer. It was also known as Jupiter's Eye or Beard. Eliza couldn't help telling her sister: "Do you know, Bec, you can never kill that old thing, but Aunt say that's wonderful good for burns."

Aunt Danbrook was a wonderful housewife and, apart from a few groceries, was almost self-contained. But there, one had need to be in a place like Eastbridge. She could even make her own candle and lampwicks out of cotton grass.

Her next-door neighbour was an old man named John Bidwell, who had been a carrier in his younger days, between Woodbridge and Ipswich. He used to have a bunch of St. John's wort hanging in his little window as a charm against being over-looked, tempests and thunder. He had made a bit of money on the side in the days when body-snatching was rife, by conveying the bodies in his cart. They were put out ready for him on the churchyard wall, he would come along, put them in his cart and cover them up with various goods. As he got near to Ipswich, doctors and students would be waiting, and he would unload. It was a tricky business, but he never got caught.

He lived to be 95 and had never had a bottle of doctor's medicine in his long life. Not likely, he had it firmly fixed in his mind that those bodies were made up into medicine, and he wasn't having anything of that. Enough for him those ghoulish jobs.

To return to Theberton. It was a great place for superstition, which may or may not have stemmed from the old abbey at Leiston. But it may have come down the ages because red, fallow and roe deer, wolves and wild boars, beavers and even bears had roamed about those parts. They believed in witchcraft and the strange subtle power of the weasel, or whitteritt, as it was sometimes called. It was extremely unlucky to meet one first thing in the morning; and one hesitated to kill it, for it might be a witch and take revenge. There was, too, an old reference in local records for 13th November 1753:

It was agreed that James Goleby the overseer, provide a place to dip Ann Clark in order to recover her of her lameness; and that he provide her with such necessaries as are needful during the time of dipping; and that he give an account of the success thereof to the Parishioners as soon as occasion require.

Years later there was to be an open-air baptism on Middleton Moor, but this dipping case at Theberton in 1753 suggests the presence of a Holy Well.

During its long history, they had had some curious parsons, to wit a Parson Fenn, and one who wrote in his Register for 1769, recording the six children of John and Martha Lord, "These six children were born quakers and christened afterwards."

Moreover, they were great bell-ringers. They used two bells for passings; for the greater bell you paid eighteen pence an hour, and for the smaller one shilling. When a parson died they tolled the larger bell for two hours. The gleaning bell was rung until the middle of the nineteenth century. It was said too, that the four bells chimed in honour of the keeper of the nearby inn, 'The Lion', "Come Tom Wal—ler, Come Tom Wal—ler!"

Among the squires was one George Doughty, who had many friends. This is what H. M. Doughty writes of him in his *Chronicles*: "Among his early intimates was one whose name is connected with Theberton. Francis Light had founded the colony of Penang or Prince of Wales Island, and became its first Governor; and loving his home land as all Suffolk men do, had given to a tract of ground the name of Suffolk."

Francis Light sent to George Doughty one of his sons and a request that Goldsberry Farm should be bought on his behalf. His finances being not equal to his ambitions, the farm was not acquired. Doughty remarks, "The farmhouse on Gouldsbury's Farm, afterwards known as the 'Brick House', was the property of a Mr. Gouldsbury, who later sold it to a Mr. Wooton."

On the establishment of a British Province of South Australia, Light was appointed Surveyor General. Having arrived, he proceeded to select the site and to lay out the ground plan of the city of Adelaide, dying there in 1838. His house there he named Thebarton, using the old spelling, and a suburb of the city bears the name of this little Suffolk village. It is said—and we may hope the custom still survives—that when a new mayor of Adelaide is elected, a silver loving cup filled with local wine is handed round, and the memory of Colonel Light is solemnly toasted.

When the Plague raged in the streets of London and spread down to Ipswich and Yarmouth, it did not touch Theberton, so delightfully detached was it from the busy world. Yet this little hamlet produced a Francis Light; Charles Montague Doughty, author of that marvellous book, *Arabia Deserta*; and a Doughty V.C. Not a bad lot for a tiny village.

No, thy Ambition's Master-piece
Flies no thought higher then a fleece:
Or how to pay thy Hinds, and cleere
All scores; and so to end the yeere:
But walk'st about thine own dear bounds,
Not envying others larger grounds:
For well thou know'st, *'tis not th' extent*
Of Land makes life, but sweet content.

Herrick

3

VILLAGE LIFE A HUNDRED YEARS AGO

••◦✿◦••

My laughter is over, my step loses lightness,
Old countryside measures steal soft on mine ear
I only remember the past and its brightness,
The dear ones I mourn for again gather near.
Traditional Welsh Folk Song.

Grandfather's farm, as I remember it with those first glimpses of consciousness that belong to childhood, was a lovely, beautiful entity of age-old buildings, rustic noises, soft outlines, gentle shadows and immortal memories. There was nothing new about it. It had always been like that, and somehow grandfather and grandmother had always been part of it. Indeed, it was an evocation as well as a creation, coming down from the feet of heaven.

Sometimes today a farm is referred to as an agricultural factory, a horrid beastly expression. As though it were an outcrop of the laboratory, rather than a flower which had sprung up by the wayside to gladden the eyes, and a fragrance to quicken and comfort the heart.

The air was still, yet full of gentle murmurings: the hurried, almost ominous passing of a fly, the positive note of a bee; and always, not far distant, the song of the sweet singing lark. All was at peace; the Hungry Forties had given place to something of prosperity; stack burning and machine breaking had long since ceased. Neither was there any rush or turmoil. The age of the commuter was not yet, for men lived and died in their own place, the village that held their names in old, old registers and sometimes on a grave-board. The fret and care of ambition stirred them not, neither did lethargy stultify their outlook. They were individuals all.

Beatrix Potter in her diary, recently decoded, wrote of the death of a certain Captain Green, the last surviving naval officer present at the funeral of Nelson. The papers mentioned at the time an odd thing, that he died in the same room and bed in which he was born. That could have been matched in many a village in Suffolk in last century.

Of course there were sluggards, and no amount of prodding would alter them. There was, for instance, Cork Beckham who only had one eye. It was said of him he had lost the other looking for work. Grandfather, a man of no education according to books and sophistry, used to say he had two ears, one to let the squit in and the other to let it out. He had a wonderful forthright language at his disposal. Of such folk as Beckham he would remark—"He don't like working atween meals." On the other hand he might describe a fussy person who did little or nothing, as having buttoned up a bumble bee in his trousers. Or another, as being so sharp "he'd cut hisself". However, at times it was almost classical, certainly Elizabethan, as when the old man exclaimed, "Har com' bright Phabe, she'll soon hussle ta corn."

Even children were under strict observation, and you need no explanation for a remark called forth by a certain gardener's boy, that his favourite occupation was "chasing snails off the garden path". Although we must remember that in those days there was no law against the use of the cane, neither could son sue his father for cruelty. Farmers and others could use their sticks across the shoulders of some poor downtrodden urchin without restraint or redress. If those 'bors' didn't get a lot of meat in their diet, there was always a good supply of 'lamb pie', which was an alias for a drubbing.

However, in this respect, I cannot do better than use the words of old Robert Reyce, writing in his *Breviary of Suffolk* in 1618:

> To come unto the persons themselves of this Country, inhabitants, when I remember their names and language, I find no dialect or idiom in the same different from others of the best speech and pronunciation. For as wee border nott upon any forreine limitts of different tongue, by whose vicinity in our common

trafficke wee have cause by encroaching upon others to diversifie
our owne naturall language; so having no naturall defect proper
to this soile, doe we disgrace that with any other broade or rude
accent which wee receive at the hands of gentility and learned
schollers, whereof wee have many trained up in the best and purest
language. Howbeit I must confesse our honest Country toyling
villager to expresse his meaning to his like neighbour, will many
times lett slip some strang different sounding tearmes, no wayes
intelligible to any of civil education, untill by the rude comment
of some skillfull in that forme, which by daily use amongst them
is familier, they bee after their manner explained. Butt this being
onely among the ruder sort, the artificer of the good townes
scorneth to follow them, when he naturally prideth in the counter-
fitt imitation of the best sort of language, and therefore noe cause
to observe any thing therein.

The Hon. L. A. Tollemache in his *Old and Odd Memories* gives
a wonderful insight into social behaviour of those times, as
carried on at Helmingham. He first quotes Augustus Hare as
giving a quaint old-world picture of the social economy of a
Shropshire parish: "The curates always came to luncheon at the
rectory on Sundays. They were always compelled to come in
ignominiously at the back door, lest they should dirty the
entrance; only Mr. Egerton was allowed to come in at the front
door, because he was a 'gentleman born'." He goes on to say:

This comical state of things bears a sort of analogy to what
occurred at Helmingham in my father's boyhood, and even in my
own. I well remember when the country doctor used to come in
at the back door, and sometimes, there being no steward's room, to
take refreshment in the housekeeper's room. Nor, a decade or two
earlier, did the rector fare much better. My father told me that,
when his uncle, Lord Dysart, was in authority, the rector, Mr.
Bellman, was on Sundays, indeed, allowed to dine with the family,
but was received with ostentatious patronage. On week-days the
physician of souls sank to the level of the apothecary; the housekeeper's room was thought good enough for him. Mr. Bellman
lived on into what many called our Evangelical era, his successor
having been the Rev. J. C. Ryle, afterwards Bishop of Liverpool.
I can just remember the aged rector in his wonted resort, the
housekeeper's room; and I fear that I must have imbibed a drop
or two of anti-clerical virus, for I am accused of having thrown the
good old man's hat into the moat, nor do I seem to have been
punished as severely as, child though I was, I deserved to be.

However, they had all kinds of happy little customs in those far-off days. Simple but deeply significant, as the gesture made by the cowman who drove his herd to the church to be baptised. In the *Ipswich Journal* for 1724, mention is made of an old inn and a Shrovetide custom:

> This is to give notice that on Shrove Monday, at the Sign of the Shears in St. Margaret's Parish in Ipswich, FIVE HOUSINGS and FIVE COLLARS, of Two Pounds Value, are to be drawn for, no less than Two Teams to draw, and to enter by Twelve of the Clock.
>
> Any Gentlemen that will favour me with their good company, shall meet with a hearty welcome from their humble servant. George Ixer.

Grandfather's village was rather low-lying, so one could not always see the church, hidden as it was by sundry little risings in the ground. But one could hear it, a peaceful happy sound expressive of joy rather than sorrow. Sorrow, or a certain awesomeness, was in that ancient steeple also, when someone died and the tenor told his or her passing. Funerals too were an event, and there was that little bit of tenderness of remembrance when the slow-walking procession stopped for a moment or two against the garden gate of a friend or relative.

The 'arly sarvice' was at eight, as now; some of the participants walking a goodly distance to be present. Sometimes their steps would be hastened because the rector might dispense the remainder of the wine to certain poor old men and women. He would know their need and be generous in his preparations; and they would be 'whooly' comforted. Besides, as far as he and his family were concerned, there were brewing tubs in his outhouses, recorded in his terrier; and a wine cellar under his old rectory that was not altogether innocent of a puncheon of strong water, that had arrived there one dark night, ferried along the little local river. Grandfather might even have had a suspicion of when it happened. But there, you couldn't touch the rector; he was a gentleman, had all kinds of learned books in his study, calf-bound with gilt enrichments. And, although he probably never read them, they looked the part, had belonged to his father before him, and helped him to become a Master of Arts of Cambridge, and a Justice of the Peace. As Percy Lubbock has so beautifully said, "What is culture? Is it not, first of all to take a mind and let it loose into the past?"

The village belfry was the one vocal point of the whole community. It had its customs and occasions as already stated. But nowhen did it sound the sweeter than at Advent, and in some cases the heralding of the New Year.

At one village the belfry had four bells, but the tenor was cracked and out of action. About 11.30 in the last hours of the old year, the rector with his son would set out for the church, carrying an old lantern that had a nasty habit of going out with every gust of wind. They were to ring out the old year, now so nearly dead, and the new year in.

The father would pull a rope with each hand, while the son managed the other. First they rang in rounds, then tolled out the old year with the passing bell, as was fitting. Now came a few minutes pause, then for five minutes they pulled the ropes fast and furiously, waking up the whole village.

On the way home they passed an old lady's cottage, who would hold up her lamp at the tiny window, as a sign she had 'heerd'. A retired admiral also joined in the little ceremony, and rang his ship's bell as they passed to bed.

Alas, Middleton bells have been silent long since, even the rector came to the days spoken of by the preacher, when

the almond tree shall flourish, and the grasshopper shall be a burden, and desire shall fail: because man goeth to his long home, and the mourners go about the street. Or ever the silver cord be loosed, or the golden bowl be broken at the cistern. Then shall the dust return to the earth as it was: and the spirit shall return unto God who gave it.

Indeed, "Vanity of vanities, saith the preacher; all is vanity", for the rectory has been alienated from the living, and the parish is served from the next village.

Some of the old parsons were renowned for their stupidity, as the one who had a knack of hanging about a farmyard and asking stupid questions. On one occasion he was watching a stockman feeding pigs. "What fine pigs, what uncommonly fine pigs, to be sure! How old may these pigs be?" he asked.

"Well, sir," replied the man looking quite serious, "I should not like to say exactly, but to the best of my knowledge they must be just on 50 years old!"

Framsden Mill

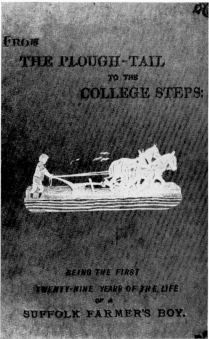

(*above*) A Suffolk backwater, Theberton. (*left*) Suffolk 'bor'.

"Dear me, who would have thought it," replied the old man. "Fifty years, did you say? What an age for a pig."

This reminds me of the story about the clerical fop, as told by François de la Rochefoucauld, when touring England in 1794. He was met with at Massingham, Norfolk.

The clergyman of this parish, we were told, is the greatest fop imaginable and consequently a very amusing character. His parishioners told us that he always comes to church with his hair beautifully dressed and powdered; but he reads so quickly and preaches so loud that it is impossible for anyone to follow him, and people come out of church they say, without knowing anything more than when they went in. The way in which he obtained his doctorate at Cambridge is unique. Having gone there to get his degree, he was asked whether the sun turned round the earth or the earth round the sun. Not knowing what to say and wanting to make some reply, he assumed the emphatic air and boldly exclaimed: "Sometimes the one, and sometimes the other." This reply produced so much amusement that he was made a doctor on the strength of this piece of fatuous stupidity.

It must be admitted that these so-called downtrodden and ignorant villagers had a sly humour, which every now and then crept out. There was a tale running about regarding a certain cleric's wine cellar that was the subject of a burglary. How the marauders got in and spirited the contents away baffled the local constable and the gentry also. They not only got in, but got the better of a vicious dog that was on guard. It was the talk of the place. Presently a few hints began to be noised abroad, and one ne'er-do-well was heard to say he knew who had the parson's wine, that he did.

Needless to say, the parson got to hear of it, as it was intended he should, and went off post-haste to the gentleman in question.

"I understand, Stollery, you know who had my wine?"

"That I do, sir," was the ready response. "You had it, but you couldn't fare to keep it."

There was also the incident of long ago concerning a rector of Stonham Aspall. The Rev. Robert Baynes held the living in 1755 and was the proud possessor of some exceedingly fine geese, which he tended in his orchard. On going to them one morning he found that all the geese were missing, save the gander, which was fluttering about, with its head apparently fixed

3

to the ground. On going to the bird he discovered that around
its neck had been tied an old-fashioned purse. This contained
some coppers and also a piece of paper, inscribed:

> Dear Mr. Baynes, do not trouble your brains,
> Or let your thoughts to wander;
> We have purchased your geese at a penny a piece
> And left the change with the gander.

Grandfather was referred to as Master, never Mr., and he
was greatly respected. He was poor but upright, and villagers
in those days were quick to apportion a man's character. There
were plenty of tricksters about, but they appreciated a man of
his word. The biggest rogues were the horse dealers, and it was
wonderful what they could do in palming off a broken-winded
and spavined animal.

> I think 'em as much in the wrong;
> As those who expect a true word,
> From a Lawyer's or Horse-dealer's Tongue.

Next came the old dealers and hucksters, with their plausible
talk. The gipsies were a race apart, and after all, they were not
village folk.

The countryman's gift of second sight was something to be
reckoned with. And they were quick on the uptake, like old
Lightskin Darkins, who was a bit of a sportsman in his way. If
he was fond of a nag, he was also fond of the Church Service
and his place in the choir.

When a little bit of an argument arose at the squat old-
fashioned pub known as 'The Bell', and Spade Rous said he
couldn't nohow make out why a man like him went to church,
Darkins up and said, "Look yew hare, partner, I'm a goin' tew
heaven my way, an' yew can go to hell your'n. So thare yew be."

There was also the man who was wont to disappear, and no
one knew where to find him. His master could stand it no longer,
so in his wrath he shouted, "Where hev yew bin? Tell me, or
I'll sack yew!"

The answer came back calm and collected, "I've bin as far
this side o' London as the other."

And they were not above taking a rise out of their betters, as
the Varsity man found to his annoyance. He liked a sprint, or at
least a quick walk in the evening. On one such occasion he

noticed he was being followed by a number of what he thought were louts, calling out, "Holler Johnson: Holler Johnson!"

He was wholly riled, pulled himself up and asked them what the hell they meant?

"Oh," said they, full of apology, "we thowt yew wur ole Johnson. Now we see yew bain't."

"Who is Johnson, then?" persisted the sprinter.

"Oh, sir, he's haf a fule who go runnin' about o'nights."

Generally speaking their powers of endurance were remarkable. Hot or cold, wet or dry, they could stick it out; and their strength was prodigious. It is usually thought the blacksmith wanted a bit of matching, but he was often outclassed by the miller. In many cases the latter was the strongest man in the village and could handle a sack of wheat as easily as some folks could cope with a bag of feathers. It was a miller who was asked to vacate his seat in church. After squaring up to the wardens he remarked, "You'll have to prove yourself a better man than me, before I come out o' this." So they let him bide.

They could trudge up and down the furrows, hour after hour, facing the wind and rain, with a stamina that seemed well nigh unconquerable. But then what must it have been like to take an outside seat on a coach in winter? Too often, however, they were brought low by the ague, the universal complaint of thost who faced the elements. And, be it remembered, 'Yarmouth mittens' was an alias for bruised or chapped hands.

Their power of strength was also seen in the harvest field, where they required stamina as well as skill. It was surprising how many old men would seek to excel in this heavy work of pitching and tossing, cutting and binding. They counted up their harvests with as much pride, as some reckoned the quarterings on their shields.

Here they faced the heat, as in hedging and ditching, ploughing and sowing they faced the cold. And they were mighty afraid of getting sunstroke or blisters on their arms, lest these should turn to blood poisoning. When the parson read out that illuminated passage from the Old Book about the "little owd bor", who got sunstroke in the harvest field and cried out, "My head! my head!" they knew all about it, even if it was in a foreign field and far away. After all, the Bible spoke to them in a living language; they understood it as we seldom do today.

In those far-off days, the men were given half a day off to go to the blacksmith's to get their scythes hung before starting the harvest. They used to mow the corn all in a row. Then they would lay down their scythes and tie up the corn in sheaves. That is a sight lost to us today.

If you want visual evidence of their stamina, go into a museum and study a surgeon's box of instruments as used in those days. He would operate without anaesthetics on men who would hardly turn an eyelid. It was the only way, and they accepted it. To us of this age of opiates, the use of these butchers' outfits call to mind the misfortunes that befell the early Christians, as recorded in the Epistle to the Hebrews: "They were sawn asunder." This sort of treatment befell my own father as a child (born 1850). He dislocated his knee-cap jumping off a heap of stones with other boys. He was taken home, placed on the kitchen table, his knee hacked about without anaesthetics, and lamed for life.

Villages were full of these tales of endurance, either at the doctor's hands or meeting some emergency. There was the case of a farmer who was roused from his sleep by noises of which he knew the import. Someone was robbing his hen roost. He out of bed in a twink, not stopping to put on shoes or stockings, trousers or jacket, and gave pursuit, dressed only in a calico shirt, on a bitterly cold night. He at last caught up with the culprit, who found himself in Ipswich jail. Of course that tale went the round of the local inns and lost nothing in the telling. Neither was the farmer any the worse for the exposure.

The ideal era of farming, according to M. Beetham-Edwards —and she ought to have known, since she was a farmer in her own right—was the middle years of the last century. These are her words:

A delicious retreat when no young colts are disporting themselves in its precincts, is the pightle (a small enclosure near the house), now a glory of cowslips, sweetest of all flowers, now of wild clover, pasturage of the bees. A breeze blows freshly even in July, there are no sultry days in my beloved Suffolk, and here also the idler would find himself alone.

That bygone pastoral, I am tempted to say pageant, has never been supplanted by richer, more varied experiences. With the reaping machine, the patent mower, the steam thresher, vanished all poetry from cornfield and farmyard. With the improved kitchener, mechanical churner, and the inroads of gentility, farmhouse life has become prosaic as that of a stocking factory. But in former days it was not so. Hardships there might be, boorishness there might be, yet the bucolic spirit from time to time reigned in these homely scenes, for a brief interval existence wore the aspect of Bacchanalia. Their ruddy faces gleaming like red-hot coals against the golden sheaves, the lusty reapers obeyed beck and nod of the 'Lord of the Harvest', leader chosen for his prowess, commanding presence, and high character generally. At a signal from the lord all filed off to the nearest hedge for bait and beaver . . . . a can of the oldest and strongest beer being supplied from the farm upon extra occasions. Decency characterized the conversation, oft-times master and men sitting down together.

And remember, the farmer wore a white smock, the labourers a brown one.

> Under the sun on the grey hill,
> At breakfast camped behind the hedge,
> There ate he, there eats he still,
> Bread and bacon on the knife's edge.

Although Miss Edwards's strictures on the mechanical side of this hard work sounds rather odd to farming ears today, the romance was there and gave rise to Bloomfield's famous song. She evidently hadn't any time for the inventions of Garrett's of Leiston or Smyth's of Peasenhall then coming up.

Women figured in the scene in all their mysterious and inspired instincts and marvellous strength of character. The Wise Woman was one, but she was not the only one. There were women blacksmiths, women publicans, even women farmers. In those now long distant days, not so much distant in time as in customs, it was no uncommon thing to see 'Mary Smith' or 'Ann Brown, Farmer', on tumbril and wagon. But they never went to market. Their samples of wheat and barley, neatly sewn up with pack thread in brown-paper bags, were exhibited either by a male relative, friend or bailiff. In the same way they purchased pigs and sheep, and sold their fat stock. Neither did they attend cattle fairs, stock sales or rent dinners. Etiquette saw to that. However, they got in their wheat early, kept their land clean, and sent prime sheep and bullocks to the fair.

Butter and eggs and poultry were sold to market women, who

called once a week. One of them on being refused part, announced huffily, "Well, Miss, since I cannot have the butter, I must *re*cline the eggs."

These would be carried to market in the old frail baskets, and, when they had been sold, the old dame would come home with a parcel of tallow candles, spices for ham pickling and canvas for the cream sieves. This last would be known as 'picklin', which was the Suffolk name for a coarse linen, and is described thus by Forby:

> A sort of very coarse linen, of which seedsmen make their bags, dairy-maids their aprons, etc. Lin is an Anglo-Saxon word for flax; from the Latin linum of course. We have it in the compound linseed; and this is another compound importing that the manufacture is from the coarser parts or *pickings* of the flax.

This reminds us that there was nothing to touch Suffolk ham, pickled in spice and harvest beer. The beer was as clear as sherry but twice as strong.

A farm was known as an occupation, and it was a much-coveted way of life, as it was a fine business for those with a little capital. It was seldom that a farmer who led a steady life failed in his undertaking. On the contrary, he might find himself suddenly rich, like the one who had the following additions to his stock in one night. His wife was delivered of a child, a cow calved two calves, three ewes yeaned nine lambs, and a sow farrowed eleven pigs. One of the latter being a 'plum-pudden-pig'.

Sometimes they found themselves a bit short of money, but they managed. And to the credit of these yeomen countrymen, they seldom or never, married for money. It wasn't done.

One farmer, unmarried, near to middle-age, who could have done with a little more capital, showed the trend. Not far away were two spinsters, well provided for, but who had not been sought after. A family council suggested he might try for one of them. After much hesitation, and in a moment of desperation, he braced himself, put on his Sunday best, had his gig cleaned and the harness polished, and drove off.

An hour or two later he was seen dashing home again in a most jubilant mood. The family rushed out to meet him at the door, the trap was led away, and he entered the house. "Thank

God!" they said among themselves. "It is settled." But their conclusion was too hasty, for, with undisguised relief, declared, "She's refused me!" So there you are, one is driven back to the old ballad:

> Women make men Love,
> Love makes them sad,
> Sadness makes them drink,
> And drinking sets them mad.

In 1832 a farmer offered his wife for sale, as it was then thought quite legal, and a number of cases were reported. However, I don't know what Suffolk farmers would have done without their helpmeets, especially when one realizes that in states of emergency women could run the concern themselves. In any case they figure in second place in the Harvest toast.

> She is a good woman, she prepar'd us good cheer,
> Come, all my brave boys, now, and drink off your beer.

Yet, of course, there was always the question of her ability to prate, which calls to mind the case of Margaret Cutting, "A young woman now living at Wickham Market in Suffolk (1742), who speaks readily and intelligently, tho' she has lost her tongue." The question naturally arises, what could she have done if she had had one?

In summing up the womenfolk, one can always fall back on the kind of epitaph of which our old churches are so full.

> Here resteth in hope the body of Rose the wife of John Glover
> parson of this Church, daughter of Humphrey Robert of
> Charsfield who died the 20th. of December Anno Dni, 1621.
>> As withered Rose its fragrant scent retains
>> So being dead her vertue still remains
>> She is not dead but chang'd, ye good ne'r dies
>> But rather she is Sun-like left to rise.

And how these old Suffolk husbandmen adored their horses! One sad occasion is recorded, where, through misfortune, a farm had to be sold, including the stock. When it came to the terrible end, there was a favourite animal of both horseman and owner. At the final act of separation, the man put his arms round the animal's neck and wept. It appeared as though the horse knew and added its tears to the parting.

The Suffolk ploughman loved his charges. If his master was of the stingy variety, he would go so far as to steal corn for them. He would think nothing of spending hours brushing and braiding their tails, and making their coats to shine; meanwhile holding a running conversation with his bosom companions.

Their wonderful way with animals is well brought out in *Life in a Norfolk Village*, published in 1949. One man, an old fisherman, turned wherryman, was said to have killed his goat with kindness, which surely was no easy task. When he grew old he looked after a few ducks. If they were not home on time he would take out his boat and go in search. His joy was complete when he turned them back homewards, "Sarve ye right. Didn't I tell ye so? And now wind and tide agin ye. How on arth are ye a goin' tew git hoome." Back they would come, gaggling all the way, as glad to see him as he them.

He also had a couple of geese who became so attached to him that when he went to Norwich they were waiting his return halfway along the village street and would give him a joyous reception. His old hens would be only too pleased to perch on his shoulders. When he passed on, quietly in the night, his two cats were found curled up at the foot of his bed in the morning.

There was also the case of a certain Storey Smith, who spent two whole days at school and no more. He evidently ignored the advice given by an old schoolmaster, in his *Reading Made Easy*:

> The boy, I am sure, does well
> Who tries to read and spell,
> And if with all his might
> He strives with pen to write
> He soon his end will gain
> Nor will he strive in vain.
> Then who would not take pains
> Since great would be his gains?
> For if you would be made
> A man of art and trade
> You both must read and write
> Or else you can't do right.

He was probably lured away by the promise of a job, for he was at work at seven years of age, scaring crows. But like many of the old shopkeepers who could neither read nor write, he was as good as a ready reckoner. He could calculate the acreage of land as well as any surveyor.

In process of time he became head horseman and a great lover of those one-time friends of man. One of his jobs was to take a stallion, named Prince, to the various farms. At his last call on one occasion, the farmer decided to celebrate the occasion and gave Storey a stiffish glass out of the black bottle. (Not, you will understand, the same thing as a black dose.) Now Storey was a plain man and drank only beer, not spirits, and it was not long before the effects were well and truly felt. He managed to sit his charge home, but when he reached the stackyard he fell off in a heap. Prince turned his head round, saw his master on the ground, made a half-turn, grabbed him by the collar and put him on his feet.

Storey's command over horses was such that he was usually called upon when there was any trouble with them. On one occasion a horse had been punished. At the first opportunity it lunged out at the farmhand who had struck it, so savagely that he was in hospital for some time. It was the same with any others who came near the horse. Storey was therefore called in. His wife implored him not to go, but he had no fear. His first move was to order the farmer out of the stable. In a few minutes, by gentle words and caresses, he had the horse eating out of his hand. However, there was only one cure for the trouble and that was to sell the horse and so dispel its grievances.

Storey Smith was a regular churchgoer, and although he was no scholar, as we have seen, yet his knowledge of the Bible was such that if half a verse was quoted to him he could complete it. And remember, that was the magnificent English of the Authorized Version, which our modern scholars want to depose.

Another member of that family exhibited a remarkable instance of pre-natal influence on the mother, leaving its mark on the child. His mother had been in service at the vicarage, where was a fine specimen of a mulberry tree. After marriage she frequently returned to her old place, and on one occasion the vicar's wife asked her to gather up some of the fruit that lay on the ground. Whilst so doing one of the mulberries fell on her head, of which she took no particular notice. When her child was born, there on his head was a tiny growth shaped like the fruit, and on the same spot as where the one had struck the mother. It remained with him all his days. But strange to relate, just as the fruit changes colour as it ripens, so that growth on his head changed also.

Country life was indeed circumscribed in those years, but folks were happy in their straightness. They fully believed the world was flat, for how else would you keep the water and the sea in its place? In one village they had a bit of a rise known as America Hill, and it was the general belief that if you climbed it and kept on walking you would get there sooner or later. Then, if you mentioned a village a few miles away, they might admit they had 'hee'rd on't', but had never been there. After all, they are not interested in foreign parts. But local pride would out, as expressed in the verses written in dialect extolling a bit of a hill at Great Totham, Essex:

> At Tottum's Cock-a-Bevis hill,
>   A sput supass'd by few,
> Where toddlers ollis haut to eye
>   The proper pritty view.
> Where people crake so ov the place,
>   Less-ways, so I've hard say;
> An' frum its top yow, sarteny,
>   Can see a monsus way.
> 'Bout this oad hill, I warrant ya,
>   Their bog it nuver ceases;
> They'd growl shud yow nut own that it
>   Beats Danbury's a' to pieces.
> At Cock-a-Bevis hill, too, the
>   Wiseacres show a tree,
> Which if you clamber up, besure,
>   A precious way you see.
> I dorn't think I cud clime it now,
>   Aldoe I uster cud;
> I shudn't warsley loike to troy,
>   For guelch cum down I shud.

Some parts even produced the best fish, always remembering the remark made by an old country philosopher: "How fish do grow when they are out of the water":

> Wytham eel and Ancum pike
> In all the world there is none syke.

Of course, they had to admit defeat sometimes, but it was rare:

> Rising was a seaport town
> When Lynn was but a marsh;
> Now Lynn it is a seaport town,
> And Rising fares the worse.

Some of them too had wonderful long memories and might tell you that "My late wife's first husband's first wife's first husband's first wife's cousin, told her he could remember the Battle of Hastings right well."

And they could be a long time coming to the point: "Wan I wur crossin' ta sax acre midda, as ta sighin is, I see ole Master Noller, as ta sighin is; yeow neow whaat I mane."

Then, of course, they were very cautious, marvellously so. For example a caller at a cottage noticed an old man sitting in the baccus (scullery) and was unwise enough to pry into details.

"So you have a visitor, Mrs. Woolnough. Some relation, I suppose?"

"Well, yes, Miss, to be sure," came the reply. "He is a little related to me. He's my father."

Naturally enough, besides their baptismal name, the men had a nickname by which they were known. It was Clock Hewett, Sheep Rising, Nobby Clarke, Dusty Miller, Crab Yaxley, Cribbage Cook, Cockey Robinson, Chucky Harris, Nobber Weston, Pink Norman, Topper Lubman, Chad Granger, Tittle-pin Sawyer, Bob-for-yer-Hog; and all the Charlies were Wags. 'Christmas' came naturally to one born on 25th December; but surely Dionysius Thain wanted a bit of beating.

Their cures were remarkable. The only thing they couldn't cope with was old age, as the man found out who accosted the doctor with, "Am I dangerously ill, sir?" "No," was the reply, "but you are dangerously old." Some of the remedies were used on us as children by my mother; and the smell is ever before me. Such as wearing a piece of camphor round the neck, or a piece of rag soaked in vinegar wrapped round the forehead as a cure for a sick headache. I can remember my mother doing that. Then, as we were homoeopaths, the recommended dose of taking as much saltpetre as would lie on a threepenny bit, would be well understood. And when it came to a tallow plaster, to be really effective it had to be a heart-shaped piece of brown paper.

There was also wintergreen ointment, adder's tongue ointment, both for open sores; and rue tea for the innards, which
was the bitterest physic of them all. If they couldn't sleep, which
was rare, they would dose themselves with henbane.

A conceited doctor might be known as the Black Dose, which
put him squat amongst his own pills and ointment. I don't know
that there were many cases of conceit, but I fear there were
several among the faculty who could be classed as bullies. But
then, they had to do with a strange race of people, who might
remark as a matter of course: "Tis funny you havin' the n'ralgar
like that." Of course it wasn't funny at all. Or, "Twas funny his
dyin' so sudden." Besides, they were on intimate terms with the
churchyard, and there might be the lament, said with great
feeling: "She went down tew hare grave wi' a bootiful set o'
teeth in er hid, all er own."

Their diseases varied from an ulster, varico or harico veins,
ammonia or harmonia, to singeing for deafness: "I'm so hard
o' hearin', I had tew git my ears singed." But a cure might be
affected by pouring in hot eel oil, or by sticking an 'ellern'
[elder] twig into the ear and wearing it three nights and a day.
"But thare, the doctor told me the bacteria 'd have to follow the
diphtheria." Or, "So's that's three things the pore little thing's
got, there's ulster and cancer and gas somethin'. I can't regularly rec'lect what the nuss said 'twas."

Loud voice from husband. "Taint cancer, that's abser, *abser*,
I tell ye."

Unfortunately, work as hard as they could, be as thrifty as
they knew how, always bearing in mind the adage, "Wilful
waste makes woeful want", the one great dread towards the
evening of life of the villager was the workhouse, alias the House
of Industry. State care for a poor and declining country labourer
held out no greater torment. However, even in such a place,
individuality of character sometimes prevailed, as was recorded
in December 1765.

In the workhouse of St. Lawrence parish, Ipswich, where he
had been maintained upwards of 40 years by the said parish, died
Goward Rich, a deaf and dumb man, aged 73. He had 19 trunks
or boxes full of articles that he had hoarded up, among which were
19 pairs of buckles, 15 razors, 8 tobacco boxes, 40 knives of different sorts, 14 forks, 27 hammers, 85 pairs of shoemaker's nippers

and pincers, 33 pegging awls, 37 awls of other sorts, 22 rasps, 97 box locks, besides the sum of £17 6. 8d. all in half-pence, and £14 11. 0d. in silver.

Despite what has been said above in eulogy of the middle years of the nineteenth century, the lot of the farm labourer was certainly hard, with a four-pound loaf at a shilling, and wages at eleven shillings a week or less, and perhaps nine or ten in family. They had little or no meat; bread and cheese and an onion made up their mid-day meal. But home-brewed beer cost about a half-penny a pint. At night the good wife would make up something of a stew, with potatoes, turnips and barley flour, all mixed up together, with a thin slice of barley bread (made by herself), to help it down.

"In bad years when the corn got damp afore we could glean it", said one of them, "the flour would be so poor that you couldn't make proper bread with it. [The gleaning cry was— 'All on! All on!'] It would be black, nearly, when it came out of the oven, and the flour made from ground wheat with barley mixed wouldn't set properly. Very often, if you opened your oven door you'd have to shut it again pretty quick, to keep the bread from running out, because all the inside of the bread had oozed out of the tins on to the oven bottom. It couldn't be wasted so you let it bake on the bottom of the oven floor to a hard flat cake, and there'd be nothing left in the tins but a thick black crust all round."

Those were the days before the steam thrasher came into vogue, when a labourer could plough and sow, reap and thrash and thatch, dress a sheep and pleach a hedge. Besides all manner of other accomplishments. Surely a remarkable list for a way of life that most people considered required no apprenticeship, training or skill.

A tremendous step forward towards alleviation came with the allotment scheme. A man might have as much as forty rods, and only by that means did life become at all reasonable. Half of this would be for barley, and they would get enough to feed a pig, besides the straw which came in for bedding and manure. Rent for this would be about a pound an acre. In these days it is incredible to recall how these allotments were frowned on by the farmers. Their argument was that a man couldn't work on the farm all day, and then make long hours of overtime on his piece of land. How the labourer existed was not the farmer's concern.

These middle years of the nineteenth century, of which I have been writing, were of great importance to eastern England. In the fifties and sixties, when the grammar schools were acknowledged to be failing, a number of county schools were set up, intended particularly for farmers' sons. One of these was at Framlingham.

Then, early in the sixties, the Prince of Wales, Edward later VII, bought Sandringham. The estate had been neglected and allowed to run down. It was in a remote position and needed a deal of attention. In twenty years the Prince put up seventy new cottages; and it was not long before other landowners took note and did the same.

Two years were of great significance. 1879 was one of the wettest years that any living man could remember. And 1889 was a year of extreme distress. Alas, the race of men, outlined in this chapter, were by that time dying out:

> When now the Cock (the Plow-mans Horne)
> Calls forth the lily-wristed Morne;
> Then to thy corn-fields thou dost goe,
> Which though well soyl'd, yet thou dost know,
> That the best compost for the Lands
> Is the wise Masters Feet, and Hands.
> There at the Plough thou find'st thy Teame,
> With a Hind whistling there to them:
> And cheer'st them up, by singing how
> The Kingdoms portion *is the Plow.*
> This done, then to th'enameld Meads
> Thou go'st; and as thy foot there treads,
> Thou seest a present God-like Power
> Imprinted in each Herbe and Flower:
> And smell'st the breath of great-ey'd Kine,
> Sweet as the blossoms of the Vine.
> Here thou behold'st thy large sleek Neat
> Unto the Dew-laps up in meat:
> And, as thou look'st, the wanton Steere,
> The Heifer, Cow, and Oxe draw neere.
> To make a pleasing pastime there.
> These seen, thou go'st to view thy flocks
> Of sheep, (safe from the Wolfe and Fox)

And find'st their bellies there as full
Of short sweet grasse, as backs with wool.
And leav'st them (as they feed and fill)
A Shepherd piping on a hill.

Herrick.

4

SUFFOLK BOR

·····✺·····

Live, trifling incidents, and grace my song,
That to the humblest menial belong. . . .
The fields his study, Nature was his book;
And, as revolving SEASONS chang'd the scene
From heat to cold, tempestuous to serene,
Though every change still varied his employ,
Yet each new duty brought its share of joy.

I have just become possessed of a little book, published in 1885, entitled: *From The Plough-Tail to the College Steps. Being the first twenty-nine years of the life of a Suffolk Farmer's Boy.* The cover is embellished by an excellent example of an old wooden plough drawn by a couple of splendid Suffolk Punches. It is written anonymously, and I question if there is another person in Suffolk who would know anything about it but myself.

A copy of this book belonged to my mother, and was amongst her treasured possessions when I was a child. I thought it looked dull and uninteresting, and as there were no illustrations I never read it. Besides, I probably thought it was too pious, which was another reason for letting it alone. Alas, it perished in the London blitz, with so much else. When the old home had a direct hit, rejuvenating an old Suffolk aunt into another lease of life (she was 84 and couldn't be kept from clambering in and out the ruins), we left it all behind, removing certain valuables. Of late years I have often thought of what we lost, and I recalled this little book, wondering what was in it. But as we had an enormous amount of clutter ourselves, we had to let it go. Life and home were uncertainties in those days. Imagine my delight when another copy suddenly came to light.

(*top*) A Suffolk village, Middleton-cum-Fordley.
(*centre*) An open-air baptism on Middleton Moor.
(*bottom*) Old Hall Farm, Felixstowe

(*left* Grandmother's garden, Rackford Farm, Middleton, (*below*) *The Cynthia*, which finished her days in the Preventive Service off Southwold

The writer refers to himself twice in the text as 'J.M.', which stands for James Mills, son of Daniel and Elizabeth Mills, baptised at Stoven St. Margaret's, 17th July, 1814. In the process of time the family came to live in our own district of southeast London, in the eighties or nineties of last century. Whether or no the author came, or if the widow and a daughter after his death, I cannot say. They were Methodists, and so were we, and Mrs. Mills was my mother's class leader. She was one of those strange, powerful, enigmatic women which the Victorian era produced in such goodly numbers, wielding an off-stage influence of considerable import, a matriarch indeed. I do not know that I ever saw her, but of her I heard with almost bated breath.

But of the book itself. James Mills was born at Stoven, a tiny village between Halesworth and Beccles, in 1814, a period, be it noted, of great significance in country life, before Waterloo was both fought and won. Geoffrey Faber in his *Jowett*, speaks of it as being

> in the heyday of rural English life, when country life achieved, at any rate in many localities, an almost miraculous social balance. A happy age, when rich and poor were in charitable company together, none too rich and none too poor, the rich giving service to the poor, the poor giving service to the rich.

I think James Mills would have subscribed to this, the taskmasters in his day too often being the tenant farmers.

Mills's father was born in August 1786 and married in 1813, aged 27. Both he and his wife were staunch Church people, so they would have attended the tiny church of St. Margaret, entering by its Norman south doorway, and, unlike the common run of village folk, both could read, certainly Elizabeth could. Daniel's grandfather was a farmer with a small property in East Suffolk. His son became apprenticed to a locksmith, took to drink, and any of the family patrimony in his possession was thus dissipated. In an endeavour to avoid creditors he went to sea and never returned, meeting his end by drinking new rum. The family of mother, three boys and an infant girl were taken to the parish workhouse. There the girl died through want of suitable food, but the boys lived on to be apprenticed to farmers in the parish. This, Mills points out, was worse than slavery as

4

the boys were the property of the masters. Although some farmers were kind, his father's master was bad. However, when the servitude came to an end he was engaged as groom at Frostenden Hall, afterwards living for two years with a Sam Crisp of Stoven. In 1813 he married, having gained from his last service what was called a 'settlement'.

James Mills the first born, describes his home thus:

> The house was an old broken-down farmhouse. It stood on the side of a Green or Common, and at the edge of a wood of about 7,000 acres, called Brampton Wood.

> Where the unmolested furse
> And the burdocks' clinging burrs
> And the briar by freedom sown
> Claim the wilder'd spots their own.

> The house had not been occupied for some years, except by sparrows, rats and spiders. Part of the roof of straw had been blown off, and the opening was covered with a rick cloth, so our first home was something like a tent. My mother has told me how, lonely and sad, she watched for my father's return during that hard and dreary winter. Seldom was anyone seen except now and then some Gipsies who had encamped in the lane by the wood.

This was not their home for long as they moved to a better house by the side of the Church, fronting on to the Church Green, and thence, when James was 2, to the old Parsonage House, Frostenden, tenanted as a double cottage by labourers belonging to the Hall.

One can imagine this removal and the upheaval of their small world, all their goods and chattels piled on to a farm wagon lent for the occasion. Somewhere in front sat Elizabeth on a low chair nursing the next arrival, and the little curious boy climbing over the bits and pieces to find his mother. She, in her pawky Suffolk manner, in order to ensure his safety, enjoined him to "Sit on the bellows and find the wind." Certainly it was a little pleasantry he never forgot.

This old Parsonage House must have been an interesting place. Stone steps led to the front door, which latter is described as being of half-glass. The house was built of oak studs, with a certain amount of carving, the windows being of diamond, leaded panes. The Mills's portion was of later date and inferior in style, with one room on the ground floor some twelve feet by ten feet, and a low-ceilinged bedroom above of the same size, which had only one window some two feet square. In this room eight children were born, and before James left home, nine people slept. Here later the father died.

To the lower room a pantry had been added, and a small place built on (backhouse) for a copper and washing. The room had a large fireplace, with open hearth for the burning of logs, but a small stove had been introduced for the burning of coal. This was flanked by a brick hob on either side, where three or four of the children spent their winter evenings in a warm corner. The wide old brick chimney and the brick oven were built on the outside. One can almost smell that country room of long ago.

James recalls that a few chaldrons of coal were collected by the farmers from the nearest sea-port at the beginning of winter and given to the poor according to their need. Daniel would get five or six bushels. This coal would have been brought from Newcastle in the old Billyboy ketches. In front of the house was an open ditch for the reception of slops, and that remained stagnant. And somewhere here stood the old tithe barn.

The water supply came from a pond or pit from which clay had been dug. In winter this was filled with drainage water from the fields; in summer it became filthy and stagnant. When this occurred water had to be fetched from the Hall pump some distance away, which naturally made it very precious. Later in years a well was dug, the wall of which was covered with very fine harts'-tongue ferns. How very strange it would appear to those old country folk if they could have envisaged the piped water which has broken that age-old tradition of well, pump and pulk. However, if the water supply was poor, the milk was good. This had to be fetched from the Hall, four pints of skimmed milk for a penny, which boiled and poured over the bread made the children's breakfast. After all, it was Fuller who said of Suffolk milk: "No county in England affords better and sweeter of this kind."

This then was their home. Rude and bare it may have been, yet it was home and its memory lingered. On Sunday nights the family would be gathered together with: "Now children, in your places." One child would sit between mother and the fire, one on the same side as father, two or three on the hobs. The Bible would be brought out, and Elizabeth would read a chapter by the aid of one slender tallow candle. Surely a scene worthy of Goldsmith's *Deserted Village*. Sunday evening was the only time that Daniel could spend with his children.

Times were hard for poor folks. The cold wet summer of 1812 was followed by a poor harvest, resulting in scarcity and high prices. Wheat was 160 shillings a quarter, barley eighty shillings, and but moderate flour was sold for five shillings per stone of fourteen pounds. Elizabeth would tell how the first two or three years of her married life they could only get barley bread. 1814 was a year of very great distress for the poor, followed by a very severe winter, when all articles of consumption were dear, wages low, with pauperism and crime on the increase. Everything was taxed, even daylight.

James recounts how that when the family budget amounted to ten shillings a week by the addition of his two shillings, he would go with his mother to shop. He recalled how carefully the remainder was spent after the *meal-sack* was paid for. It was an ounce of tea, half a pound of sugar, half a pound of candles, half a pound of soap; and sixpence deposited for some much-needed article of clothing. Occasionally they had a letter which cost eightpence or ninepence, which would be reflected on next Saturday night's shopping when butter or sugar would have to be halved. When the fishing season was over, father would go to Lowestoft and buy 200 or 300 'pieces' of fish that had been bitten by the dogfish. These were generally sold cheap and would serve the family through the winter, with less butter or cheese. From these savings each one of them in turn was promised a new pair of boots or other article of clothing. It appeared they never wanted for bread, but with ten in family distress was often at the door.

It is a curious reflection on the rigid economy as recorded above that in later years Beatrix Potter could recount in her private journal: "that the labouring classes do actually suffer from miserable wages of eleven shillings a week, their unsanitary cottages, *their appalling families and improvidence*." But, of course, she had lived a cloistered life.

The after effects of the Napoleonic Wars fell very heavily on poor shoulders. It has been ever thus. In 1820 there was very great distress among the people, with everything taxed to pay the War Debt, or, as it was called, "the redemption of the debt". True, the price of wheat was reduced to sixty shillings per quarter, but farmers lessened their expenditure by dismissing their men. It was now that the odious law of 'settlement' came into operation and was strictly enforced. The two years' servitude at Stoven, where he was apprenticed, had caused Daniel to belong to that parish. Men were out of employment and were sent on the roads to work, but then they had to be paid out of the County Cess. This led the farmers to hunt out every man that did not 'belong', so Daniel had to go to his parish, and, although the rule was relaxed for him after a year or two, yet in 1826 he had finally to leave Frostenden Hall, and from that time he had to walk two or three miles to his work, and the same at night when his long day's work was done.

This interference with the law of demand and supply caused great suffering and dissatisfaction among the labouring class. For instance, Daniel's old master at Frostenden wanted him back, where he had been a trusted night-watchman, while his new master at Stoven did not want him, but was compelled to find him work. Nor did other labourers want to be removed to find him a place.

Both in 1820 and 1821 there were many riots in Suffolk. The corn drill and the threshing machine had been invented, and it was feared that these would supersede manual labour. Barley had always been sown by hand, wheat, peas and beans dibbled; this gave employment to women and children. Corn was threshed out by the flail. The first threshing machine was a tread-mill worked by men, but the new invention of using horses as the motive power caused great discontent. Men rebelled against this and were not willing to give up the time-honoured flail that gave employment 'in the dry' during the winter months.

Men out of work would gather into clusters, speeches were made, and secret conspiracies prevailed. Orders were given to destroy machinery; and they would meet for this purpose, every man with a weapon, stick, hammer, axe, pick or saw.

On one occasion the youthful James, on his way to school, saw these men at work, fifty or sixty strong, standing round a threshing machine at the Hall, their weapons in the air. At the word of command they all came down at a crash, and in half an hour, the machine was destroyed. He remarked they were running helter-skelter to the next farm.

Death came to Daniel Mills by means of one of those pulmonary diseases then so common, and his treatment by the local doctor is of considerable interest. One cold January day in 1837 (the year of Victoria's accession), he was employed in putting up faggots of furze and brushwood on rails that surrounded the horse yard. The horse pond came up to these rails and he got his feet wet, and remained in that condition all day. In consequence he caught a severe cold, which turned to inflammation of the lungs. The doctor was sent for but did not come and when he did proceeded to bleed the patient, persisting in this practise until he had "bled him to death". No wonder many of these old folks preferred the ministrations of the Wise Woman, designating the vet as 'doctor' and the man of medicine as 'Mr.' And no wonder the doctor's trade sign was a red lamp. He died on 30th January 1837 and was buried on 4th February, four of his fellow workmen acting as bearers.

It might be pointed out that this was still the age of folk-medicine, when every old woman had a charm or cure for the ague. One said, "Catch a young frog by the tail, cut off one of its feet with a flintstone, sew it up in a piece of wash-leather, and wear it about your neck night and day, and it will drive away the ague." The failure of this charm was always attributed to the neglect of some part of the instructions.

Another said, "Take a nail and hammer, go to some stile dividing a field from the road, and before it is light in the morning drive the nail into the top of the stile, but leave a part projecting. But be sure that no one sees you, or it will not cure." James laconically adds, "There were other reasons for not being seen in doing this trick."

The tale of that old country home is somewhat contradictory, as told by James, but it is revealing nonetheless. He speaks of his father's uprightness of character, and how on one occasion only they were compelled to house a cask of Hollands for the night. Elizabeth disapproved, and Daniel was ill at ease until it was gone, his comment being: "Character is more than money." James speaks of the treachery, brutality and violence of the smugglers; and after all they were near the coast.

Daniel had a house and garden for £3 a year, and, although

his wages varied from eight shillings to ten shillings a week, he had brushwood for the brick oven, milk at a nominal price, wheat for their own consumption, barley for the pig at less than market price, the gift of a few bushels of coal in winter and a kindly interest from the Hall when any of the family were sick. And James adds, "Indeed I believe there was at this time, where deserved, mutual confidence and respect between master and man." Which is confirmation of that heyday of country life referred to earlier in this narrative, for the relationship between Hall and cottage was of great significance.

Indeed, James had much cause to speak well of the Hall, for it was from the hands of one of its young ladies that he had his first remembered dose of medicine, a strong decoction of Peruvian bark to cure the ague, then so prevalent. He decided in his youthful mind not to have that complaint any more as the cure was worse than the ailment. And it was a 'Miss H.', also from the Hall, who helped him with his reading.

James's description of his age-old village church with its round tower is of great interest, as showing the condition of so many country churches at that time. It was "plain and bare inside as any building could be, with brick floor, bare walls". Not even adorned with

> mural tablets, every size
> That woe could wish, or vanity devise.

"There were plain oak and elm pews and benches, a pulpit to match, with a black cushion for the Bible; an unadorned Communion table, having no cloth save a white one three times a year." But he failed to notice the fifteenth-century font cover over the fourteenth-century font, or the two very fine fifteenth-century traceried benchends and poppy heads that were later to be made into a prayer desk. I expect folks shook their heads and said they were all as old as old could be, and left it at that.

The Hall pew was near the chancel and between it and the altar steps was a space about fifteen feet square for the children of the poor. Some of these sat on forms, some on the chancel steps. An old agricultural labourer was in charge of these with a half-rod pole in his hands as his badge of office and staff of correction. This collection of children was misnamed a Sunday School. The only lesson attempted was the Collect for the day, read over and over again till some few could repeat it. They were also taught to sit still, and woe to the unlucky wight that could not. The half-rod pole would come down on his head to some effect.

On Sunday, for a quarter of an hour, the three bells rang out from the old round steeple, calling the people to church. Most of them, however, had assembled before this to hear and exchange the news of the week, for in those days there were no newspapers. Then the parson (the youngest son of a baronet known locally as "Master Gewch"), would ride up to the gate on horseback, and the people trooped into church. The prayers and sermon were then hurried through, no part of the service proving of greater interest to the children, than the ascription to the Trinity, because then as now "the belly hates a long sermon".

Then the old man would place his pole in a corner, take out a box from a drawer and give a half-penny to each one who had arrived in time and behaved. This was comparable to another instance of which I heard. A simple woman who was given sixpence as and when she attended the *arly sarvice*. When a stranger officiated he asked what she was waiting for?

And so master James went to school. It appears that one day when playing with his sisters in the path leading to his home he heard the clatter of horses' hooves. Presently a gentleman called out, "Here, boy, hold my horse!" But the boy was scared of too close an acquaintance with a horse and tried to do the job with a stile between himself and the animal. The rider would not have this. "No," said he, "get over and hold it." For this service James received a penny. (I remember my mother telling of doing a similar job for the same fee. But her penny went into the Missionary Box.)

It appears it was the parson, come to see about James and his sister going to school, to start the very next day. He was then nearly 6.

The school, some mile and a half distant, was kept by a widow in her cottage home. And the schooldays as far as the boy was concerned lasted no longer than a year and nine months. He had learned to read before he was 5, taught partly by his mother and the lady at the Hall, and when the parson examined them at church he won the prize. This was a small book called *The Pedlar*. One paragraph he never forgot: "A gentleman looking out of his bay-window, saw a pedlar with a basket of ribbons to sell. 'Do you want any ribbons?' 'No!' At the next house, 'No!' and so on all down the street; he sold no ribbons, but the gentleman observed he kept on whistling."

The curriculum at the school included reading and writing, with 'tasks' once a week. This he discovered later was an outline of English Grammar, with the noted example:

> Tommy was a *good* boy,
> Sammy was a *better*,
> But Harry was the *best* of all.

His progress in reading was such that the parson awarded him first prize, which was no less (or more) than Leslie's *Short and Easy Method with the Deists*. Poor little boy he didn't know what it was all about, but it was a prize, to be shown and admired. Early in the spring, when he was 7 or 8 years old, he left school and was put to work. It was all written on the old jug:

> Swiftly see each moment flies,
> See and learn be timely wise,
> Every moment shortens day,
> Every pulse beats Life away,
> Thus thy every heaving breath,
> Wafts thee on to certain death.

Part of his way to school was along the London–Yarmouth turnpike, used by the coaches. In the morning they met the *Telegraph* carrying the night mail down; and at night the *Star*. These had relays of horses every ten or twelve miles. He remembered that a white horse and Fetter Lane, London, were painted on behind. The children ran after these coaches, creating an exciting game to help along the way.

Near the old home was a lane, evidently one of those old sunken roads or lokes, that was said to be haunted by one of those old coaches, running without horses. But this only happened at midnight, when he was asleep in that crowded room. He thought that one day it might run out of time, and he would see the old *Telegraph* trundling along of its own accord.

Schooldays over he transferred to Wrentham Sunday School, where he was able to continue his reading if nothing else. On Easter Monday the scholars walked in procession to Benacre Hall, every child carrying a handful of spring flowers—cowslips and daffodils, which they scattered in front of the Hall and then sang. The family stood on the balcony to listen to the children's voices. This done they marched back to school for a bun and a mug of tea, each providing his or her own drinking vessel. When he left this school he was presented with a Bible, inscribed:

James Mills,
a Gift
from the Wrentham
Sunday School.
Dec. 18, 1826.

The little fellow's working life followed the pattern set by so many centuries before. Daniel came home one night at the beginning of March, 1822 to tell his little boy, not yet 8 you will recall, that he must go with him the next morning to "keep crows". James is alleged to have wondered how he was to do this. He had heard it said about not very bright people that they had "tried to hedge the cuckoo in", and he wondered if he was to try something similar. He was up early on that first morning, between five and six o'clock, ate a hurried breakfast and trudged off behind his father, two miles of slush and mud, to a field of early sown peas. There he was left after having been told what to do. As the father's figure disappeared in the dawning light, so the poor little chap realized he was alone and burst into tears. For a week of such work he was paid one shilling and sixpence, a most valuable addition to the weekly budget. Fifty years later he went back to the spot where his father had built him a little shanty to shelter from the rain.

So early in the morning,
Before the break of day.

His next employment was driving horses at plough. While the land was wet both the horses had to walk in the furrow. He had to drive the forehorse. Then came weeding the standing corn, picking spear grass, keeping cows, picking stones; but *keeping* crows was more irksome than these.

The law of settlement was relaxed, and father returned to Frostenden Hall as a day labourer; and soon James was at work there too, at the advanced wage of fourpence a day. When he was 10 he was promoted to houseboy, or, in the colloquial language of the time, backhouse-boy. This entailed helping in the kitchen, going errands, taking care of the poultry, gathering up the eggs, fattening and killing the fowls for the table, fetching and posting the letters, for they were a mile and a half from the nearest post office and they had no walking postman. Later he was given a donkey to ride for this purpose. His hardest work, he considered, was churning the butter and making cheese. His wages were two shillings for a week of seven days.

In the winter of 1826 he was promoted to 'shepherd's boy', with sixpence a week increase. This entailed sheepfolding, marking, washing and shearing. He also worked amongst the pigs and cattle, feeding the fat pigs with barley-meal and milk morning and evening, and seeing that the milch cows were well kept and fed. His next promotion was to feed the fat beasts for the London market, and for three winters he had charge of a 'yard' of these fattening beasts. This meant keeping the yard well littered with straw, cleaning and cutting the turnips, and keeping the beasts in food. For the first time he became acquainted with the Dutch beetroot or mangel-wurzel. When roots were scarce, oil-cake was used.

In the winter of 1828 he was promoted to the 'home-yard', where the best beasts were fatted. His wages of three shillings a week were doubled in harvest, two boys doing the work of one man. His day was from light to dark for seven months of the year, which was a case of as soon as he was up he was at work, and as soon as he was in bed he was asleep.

One incident which he records is unfortunately only too typical of the hardness of so many of those old tenant farmers.

> In that summer I was employed in picking grass in a field on what was called the 'Old Meeting House Farm'. It was a fallow field and had been ploughed and harrowed to get the roots of the couch-grass to the surface, which had then to be picked up and carted off, or burnt on the field. . . . A man had charge of eight or ten boys who were kept close to their work. They were not allowed to stand up to rest their backs. I was caught by the master standing up, and, in a rage, he sent me home.

That proved to be the end of his career as a farmer's boy at the Hall Farm, for his father thought it time he was placed out at service and ease the overcrowding of that one room up in which a father, mother and eight children slept.

On 18th October 1829 James went to his new home, which was no further away than Stoven, where he had been born. He was rather proud of himself, in a large house, a large bedroom and with a large table well supplied. His master was a kind man but given to drink. When the fit was on he would not come home until midnight, and poor little James had to sit up and take his horse to the stable. Sometimes James had to go to the 'Cherry Tree', to persuade him to come home. He would then make the lad ride behind him with the horse going at full gallop, both riders and horse swaying to and fro, expecting every minute to be in the ditch.

But there was a great compensation in these long evenings, for Isaac Chenery, the farmer (an old Suffolk name), had a collection of books, amongst them *Roderick Random*, *Gulliver's Travels* and *Robinson Crusoe*. There had not been much time in James's working day from five in the morning until eight at night for reading, but the enforced vigil started him on his reading life. Certainly these volumes must have given him a new outlook, and one can imagine how they were enjoyed. However, at the end of 1830, he removed to another farm, the one where he had started work as a little boy and where the master was strict. He was not allowed to go any distance save on Sunday to church. Once again his reading time was severely curtailed, but his thirst for knowledge had been aroused, and he would hide any books he could get hold of in the hay of his pony stable. That pony took rather a lot of cleaning.

The end of 1831 saw yet another move, this time to a farm on the Stoven Middle Green, kept by a John Newbury. Here was another good master, who had been land steward to Sir Thomas Gooch, while his wife had been house-keeper at Frostenden Hall when James was kitchen-boy there. His wages now rose to £4 a year, and his day commenced at four o'clock. He commented on the diurnal round thus.

> The farmer's boy at all seasons had the care of the fowls, he had to feed the pigs, to 'tent' the cows, to wean the calves, and to be at the call of anyone who wanted a boy. If anything went wrong he was always to blame, and often the scapegoat of others' sins. In addition I had charge of the road nag, to clean and feed, and, when wanted, to harness, and often to drive it. During this year spring-carts were taxed, but farmers' market carts and those used for business were exempt, on condition that the owner's name, trade, and place were painted in full in two-inch letters behind.

I asked to be allowed to do this painting, which was my first attempt in that direction.

This calls to mind a spoonerism made by one Suffolk farmer at this time. He transposed, *Amos Todd, a taxed cart*, into *A most odd act, a taxed cart*.

He had now learned to plough, and the rule was to be in the field in winter by daylight, in summer by six. Breakfast in winter was a basin of boiled milk and in summer new milk. His description of the farmer's year is worth recounting:

As soon as spring came, or as soon as we could get on the land, spring sowing began. On the farm the order of cropping was what was called the 'four-years course'. First, wheat on one-fourth of the arable land; this was sown, if possible, in the autumn, if not, as early as possible in the spring. Second, to follow wheat, the land was well worked and cleaned for turnips, carrots, mangel etc. If one piece could not be got clean in time, it was fallow for the year, or, in autumn, cole-wort was sown for the spring feeding of sheep. Third, after turnips came barley, oats and rye, or any spring-sown crop. Fourth, one half of the quarter was sown with beans, peas, and vetches. On the other half would be clover, trefoil, etc, for hay: experience having taught that clover would not 'come' [using the old expression, butter was said to 'come'], or grow only about once in eight years.

Next in importance to sowing seed was getting the land ready. One-fourth of the land occupied all the summer in ploughing, harrowing, rolling and cleaning. Hence this was called 'summer-land', and if not sown late with turnips, was the 'fallow summer-land'. In June the hay harvest would begin, this was always a busy and anxious time. If the grass was not cut when ripe the hay would be of an inferior quality, but the state of the weather must be watched, for when the hay was made, rain would soon spoil it, and the farmer might have his winter stock of food for the horses and cattle destroyed.

The turnips were now sown and watched with much anxiety. A shower of rain would bring up the seed, and if the weather was calm, the fly would attack the young plants, cut out the crown, and, in a few days, destroy the crop and render another sowing necessary. Old May Day, May 14, new style, the horses and cows were turned out to grass. Hay and turnips had been carefully economized till this date. Now for a month or six weeks the farmer's boy had his mornings and evenings for games and recreation. My game was arithmetic, and my place of study the hay loft.

Hay-harvest over, the corn would be getting ripe. During favourable years, in the last week of July, but generally the first week in August, the harvest would begin. . . . When the day was fixed to begin, every man and boy would meet in the field at five o'clock. When all were stript and ready, the 'Lord' would give the sign, he would hold up the sickle in his right hand and say in a loud voice: "God speed the sickle, and give us health", then a dash was made at the corn. . . . Breakfast at eight, a horn of ale from the master at eleven, and dinner at twelve. Oh, the luxury of half an hour's sleep under the shade of a tree. At four o'clock another break occurred, a 'Fourses cake', and a horn of ale; this was generally brought by the master or the maid-servant, who wanted to see the harvest-field. At seven o'clock all labour ceased, except at carting-time, when we went on till dark. One man was appointed 'hornsman'; he had a tin horn about two or three feet long, which he sounded a few minutes after seven. On a calm evening the horns from many farms round would be heard at this hour. In those days few had watches, so that the horn told the time of the night to all the country round. [I wonder where all these horns have gone?]

Harvest over, the turnips had to be hoed, the second crop of clover mowed for hay, and the stubble got off the land. In ploughing for wheat, the weather must be watched, as autumn sowing would now begin, which required all the experience, judgement and energy the farmer could bring to his work, for if put off too late, it might require spring sowing, and this would make a late harvest.

At the end of two years James was offered the position of 'headman'. He was only a lad of 18, and he naturally thought it wonderful to have charge of the finest team of horses in the parish, and by far the finest set of harness. To say nothing of the responsibility of superintending all the work. He was dubious, however, so he asked his father. The offer was repeated at double pay and he accepted. These are his words concerning this position.

It was a grand day for me when I first took out my team of four fine horses with a load of wheat to Beccles market. I was up at three o'clock, the horses required extra care, the harness to be cleaned, the brasses to be polished, and the wagon to be made thoroughly respectable. I knew, as I drove out of the yard, that every one would be looking at me and my turn-out. Call it pride if you will, but as I drove away from the barn that morning and heard my kind master say to me, "May peace be with you", or

"May you return in peace", no one was happier than I. My master soon knew that I returned in peace, at the right time, with my horses fresh and nice.

It was expected of me, as headman, that I should set up the stacks of hay and the round ricks of corn during harvest. I had had no experience but I determined to do it. My master said my stacks did me credit. The custom was to build them over a little so that the water from the eaves was thrown off the stack. The great danger was that this should be in excess one side, and so endanger the stability of the ricks. In that case, it had to be propped, and farming men would say of inferior work so assisted, "Its ready to walk away."

James Mills lived in a very interesting period, but he would have been quite unconscious of the fact. Agricultural life was changing, giving way to the Industrial Revolution that was to change the face of England. He certainly welcomed these changes, and speaks with pleasure of how farming methods were changing from those as shown in the Luttrell Psalter. He remarks how the old wooden plough had given place to Ransome's Iron Patent Plough; and agricultural societies, exhibitions and prizes had stimulated man's oldest industry into a new life. Too, he had been born into the stage-coach era, and yet before he had advanced far into maturity railways had begun to run all over the land. He had heard talk of this wonderful invention, when coaches would run without horses. Although when he finally left home for London in 1843 he went by carrier's cart to Ipswich and then by the *Orion* steamer to Nicholas Wharf. But later he was to dilate on how he had travelled over 200,000 miles on the railway without accident. It is a curious reflection that a century has seen the railway that ran so close to his village home the subject of closure because of obsolescence.

When his father died he was 23, a young man at the very crown of his farming career. It reflects great credit on him that he was resolved that his mother and her still dependent five children should not go into the workhouse. This resolve was carried out, and no change in his life was made without consulting her, with this end in view. One would have thought that such proficiency in following the soil would have kept him in that way of life, but such was not the case. "What," said the oldest labourer on the farm, "give up a good place like yars, an' be a schulemaster?" By self-education and industry in acquiring learning, using a hay-loft as his study, he became a school-master and was able to impart to others something he had never heard of at his Dame's school, viz, "Numeration, Addition, Subtraction and Multiplication"; even to dividing 42,749,467 by 347. And so, as the narrative records, he came to London, presumably entered a teachers' training college, of which he says nothing, not even the 'steps'; married, had ten children, of whom seven grew to maturity, all well educated and three sons in professions. (I believe one of these was a doctor and died young of T.B.)

This career was in striking contrast to another, which has just come to my notice, concerning another son of the soil living within James's own district. In 1836 Robert Foster Woolner, farming at Mount Pleasant Farm, Dunwichw, as anxious to own his own land. This he could not do in the remnants of that ancient and drowned Borough, so he emigrated to Prince Edward Island, where he became possessed of 400 acres. There was himself, his wife and nine children, and they took with them some of their old Suffolk furniture, horses, farm implements and *seed*. It is said the variety of barley they imported was in general use in the island until recent years.

The voyage took seventy-two days, they were becalmed for a month, and food for the horses ran out; but they kept them alive on biscuits and beer. So a new piece of Suffolk grew up in a beautiful, peaceful farming countryside near the sea, like to the old home they had left behind but which was to them forever England.

ECCENTRIC SUFFOLK PARSONS

·••❧••·

Still he preserves the character of a humorist, and finds most pleasure in eccentric virtues.

Goldsmith

It is hardly necessary to describe an eccentric, although the dictionaries go to some length to do so. Suffice it to say that amongst the many meanings and explanations given are these: "Erratic, irregular, odd". But then Suffolk villages were full of such people in the days when individuality was allowed, that is before regimentation made us all alike; and the parson, the one public figure next the squire, was often the oddest of the lot.

They are alleged to have had one at Pakefield who gave rise to that very old song of many verses, which the old beach companies used to sing in chorus, especially the refrain:

> The Roaring Boys of Pakefield,
> O, Nobly do they thrive!
> They had but one poor parson,
> And they buried him alive.

> And they buried him alive—
> But a new man rose that day,
> A good one-bottle sober man
> As all the gossips say.

The tale runs that the parson had been to Lowestoft and imbibed too freely. He was walking home along the sand when he came over giddy and fell near the water's edge. The incoming tide revived him sufficiently to crawl almost to the Score (a narrow alley running down to the beach peculiar to this part of the coast), where he fell asleep. Later, two of his parishioners saw a sodden bundle lying there, went to investigate, and were horrified to discover it was their own parson. They placed the body in a hollow, threw a little sand over it, and went back to the sleeping village to blaze the news. They then proceeded to collect an undertaker, constable, lanterns and such like gear, and returned to bring home the dead. Imagine their astonishment to find the old man sitting up in his hole, spluttering sand out of his mouth and using very un-clerical language.

Amongst the rectors of Halesworth, Suffolk, in the years of the Regency, was a certain Richard Whately, who became Archbishop of Dublin. The tales concerning him are legion. He was a tutor of Oriel College, Oxford and a friend of John Keble, Pusey and Newman.

It has been said that during Whately's incumbency of Halesworth, the saintly John Keble visited him with the rough draft of *The Christian Year*. It appears that John Keble was of a Suffolk family. He may have lived and died at Hursley, but his roots were in Suffolk. Moreover, it was at Hadleigh, Suffolk, where Hugh James Rose was vicar and Dean of Bocking, that the first *Tracts for the Times* emanated. That set in being the High Church Party and the Oxford Movement.

John Keble was a remarkable man. He gained a double first at Oxford, when he was only 18, an almost incredible achievement. And from his rustic retreat at Hursley, he wielded an astonishing influence on the Church of his birth. He even suggested that if he had given more thought and attention to Newman, the latter would never have left the Church of England. Certainly Whately was one of his friends, but whether he had any influence over such a gentle person as Keble seems rather doubtful. It would seem that Pusey was of far more influence than Whately.

In the early summer of 1827, Keble's letters to various friends were accompanied by a small, plain, anonymous volume, published by Parker of Oxford. That little volume was *The Christian Year*. The little book met with instant success, and as late as 1893, when the tide of Literary fashion had already turned, it was regarded by scholars as a masterpiece. It is difficult today to even find a second-hand copy.

For long years enough, Keble was content to act as a curate to his father, in the obscure but lovely parish of Hursley, near Southampton. He was noted for his saintliness and sincerity. He could have had the highest tutorial positions at Oxford, but he preferred the quietness of a country parsonage. And it was from such an atmosphere that the ethos of the Oxford Movement was worked out. The contention was, that if the Church of England was to vanish, as the Churches of Byzantium and Ephesus have vanished, still the Church Catholic and Apostolic would live on, and the gates of hell could not prevail against it. It was not surprising therefore, to find Keble hearing the confessions of such men as Pusey, but it is astonishing to discover that the rough farm labourers of Hursley would also come to him for the same purpose.

It is said the children of the parish were his special concern. No matter how much work he had on hand he spent an hour every morning and afternoon teaching in the village school. But, be it noted, that curious little rustic touch of squirearchy; he never hesitated to put his stick across the shoulders of any who neglected to touch his cap to the vicar. After all, those were the days of that period hymn, written within sight of that lovely village of Dunster and its Castle:

> The rich man in his castle,
> The poor man at his gate,
> God made them high and lowly,
> And ordered their estate.

In Lambert's Records of Halesworth, we see something of the Keble connection with that old market town. The following charities were left, viz: "James Keble by will dated 27 Jan. 1650, left the trustees a pightle (a small enclosed field near the house), to the intent that the trustees should with the rents yearly, at or before Christmas, distribute bread to the poor of Halesworth." Also: "John Keble by will dated 16 May, 1652, left lands in Holton, half the revenue to be used in the relief of widows, and the other half to bind out poor apprentices."

In the North Chapel there is a small brass inscribed: *"Hic Jacent* Johanna *Crosse nuper uxor* Johis Crosse Gen & Maria Keble *Duae filiae* Jacobi Keble *Gen quae sepeliebantur annis Dni* 1644 & 1645."

James Keble the father of the two ladies above named, died in

1650 and his bequest to the poor of Halesworth has been already mentioned. His hatchment hangs in the vestry, and his stone is thus inscribed: "Jacobi Keble, *Depositu Servo*, *Obiit* 8 March; *ann: Era Christiania* 1650. *Aetatis Sua* 68."

Moreover, a Robert Keble was a signatory at the Court of Homage to Diana, Lady Alington, widow, mother and guardian of the most noble Egidus, Lord Alington, held on the 22nd July 1685.

Turning back to John Keble and the men of Oriel, according to Georgiana Battiscombe:

> The more predominating personality was Whately, a big blustering man of gargantuan appetite, who would tramp round Christchurch meadows hurling sticks and stones for the amusement of a large pack of dogs following on his heels. Whately was not altogether a welcome visitor in Oxford drawing-rooms. On one occasion, when calling on a young bride, he sat himself down on a new and beautiful, but not very stalwart chair: An ominous crack was heard; a leg of the chair had given way; he tossed it on the sofa without comment, and impounded another.

Again:

> The high and mighty Dr. Whately had so little consideration for the less-intelligent young men that when conducting their tutorials he would lie prone in the depths of a huge sofa with his legs dangling negligently over the back. His clever pupils he pulverized with remorseless argument and repartee, "holding them up", as he expressed it, "by one leg like dogs of the King Charles' breed to see if they squawk."

Such was the gentleman who came to Halesworth and left behind a volume of anecdotes, mostly surrounding his peculiar behaviour. One of his foibles was a certain amount of indifference to women, and in speaking of one district-visiting lady at Halesworth to another, he remarked she was "an old cabbage". This, of course, got to her ears, as well it might, and the offended lady took the rector to task. But his wit was equal to any occasion, and he parried it off with, "So you are, my dear madam—all heart."

One year his orchard suffered depredations at the hands of the local youth. He quickly put them to rights; dressed in his surplice, he hid himself in a large elm tree. When the scrumpers arrived, out he came, his gown over his head, waving his arms about. They were 'whooly' scared and made off as hard as they could go. They declared they had seen 'suffin' round Parson's Lane and Fen Farm 'midders'.

The rectory at Halesworth is a fine old Elizabethan house with a moat, and it is rumoured that when Keble went to see Whately it was while they were boating on this moat that Keble produced his work. Whately immediately recommended publication.

Whately went straight from Halesworth to Dublin and soon began to act with his usual grace of conduct. At the Privy Council he used to stand the whole time before the fire, warming his posterior, excluding the heat from others. One poor old man who was bald used to keep his hat on his head, which called forth a witticism: "A bishop keeps uncovered that which ought to be covered, and a peer keeps covered that which ought to be uncovered."

At the vice-regal lodge he made a dead-set on the drawing-room chairs, which seems to have been his hobby. He would draw over an arm-chair to the fire, stretch his legs until they reached the mantelpiece and endanger some article of virtu. He would then give full force to his arguments, and no less than four or five chairs would be put out of action with his performances of making his chair spin round on one leg. The marchioness, however, was up to these capers and landed him with a chair as heavy as lead and as firm as a rock.

Apparently he suffered with violent headaches, but had his own way of dealing with these, as this tale shows:

The first occasion on which I ever saw Dr. Whately was under peculiar circumstances. I accompanied Dr. Field to visit professionally some members of the Archbishop's household at Redesdale. The ground was covered by two feet of snow, and the thermometer was down almost to zero. Knowing the Archbishop's character for humanity, I expressed much surprise to see an old labourer man in his shirt sleeves felling a tree 'after hours' in the demesne, while a heavy shower of sleet drifted pitilessly on his face. "That labourer", replied Dr. Field, "whom you think the victim of prelatical despotism, is no other than the Archbishop, curing himself of a headache. When his Grace has been reading or writing more than ordinarily, and finds any pain or confusion about the central organization, he puts both to flight by rushing out with an axe and slashing away at some ponderous trunk. As soon as he finds himself in a profuse perspiration, he gets into bed and wraps himself in Limerick blankets, falls into a sound slumber, and gets up buoyant."

Whately was sceptical of drugs and agreed with Dryden:

> Better to seek the fields for health unbought,
> Than fee the doctor for a nauseous draught.

It was evident that, notwithstanding his avowed admiration of the gifted woman who was his wife, Dr. Whately held no high opinion of ladies, intellectually considered. Such jokes as, "the difference between a looking glass and a lady" were always welcome at his fireside. The answer was: "One reflecting without speaking, and the other speaking without reflecting."

However, he was not above telling the tale about his wife visiting a haberdasher's shop and asking for some goods in the window to be sent home. The draper was of the surly variety and refused to do so. "Sir, I am the Archbishop's lady," said Mrs. Whately, much hurt and surprised. "I don't care if you are his wife," replied the shopkeeper.

Whately's tastes were extremely simple and unostentatious, unlike those of his predecessor, Dr. Magee, who loved display. The doctor hated parade and pomp, and could not abide the gilded decorations in the palace at Stephen's Green, which cost Magee a great deal of money. Whately had no sooner taken possession of his palace, than he threatened to have the walls whitewashed, which to some extent he did in the dining-room.

But he had a most excellent side, that of doing good by stealth, because of which much could be forgiven him. The power of his intellect was great, but the munificence of his charity was greater. Those generous disbursements were all the more remarkable from the ardour with which he always inculcated principles of economy. One of the copy heads supplied by him to the children of the National Schools was, "A penny saved is a penny gained." His charity was also the more striking from the pertinacity with which he always laboured to disprove the merits of "good works".

A clergyman who made a touching appeal to his generosity was unhesitatingly accommodated with a loan of £400. He deserted the archbishop's levees, and was not seen at the palace, or heard of for many years after. One day Dr. Whately's study door opened noiselessly, and the borrower stood before him, presenting an aspect half suggestive of Lazarus and the Prodigal Son. "Halloa!" exclaimed the archbishop, starting up to kill the fatted calf, "what in the name of wonder became of you so long?"

"I did not like to present myself before your Grace," replied the clergyman, who was a man of high literary attainments and of higher principle, "until I found myself in a position to return the sum which you so generously lent me." Saying which, he advanced to the study table and deposited upon it a pile of bank notes.

"Tut, tut!" said the archbishop, taking the arm of his visitor, "put up your money; and now come down with me to luncheon."

A ripe scholar and gentleman died in Dublin, leaving his family almost destitute. Dr. Whately, having been made acquainted with the circumstance, aided them by the then munificent sum of £1,000. A classics teacher was threatened by a legal execution. Someone on his behalf, represented his painful situation to the archbishop, who, having been informed that £250 would make him a comparatively free and happy man, filled in a cheque for that amount, and thus averted a castastrophe.

At a meeting of the Irish Zoological Society, when a subscription among the members was on foot, it was suggested that the archbishop's name should be put down for at least £50. "He has not got it," interposed a member. "No one knows him better than I do. He gives away every farthing of his income, and so privately is it bestowed, that the recipients themselves are the only witnesses of his bounty."

Dr. Whately's generosity to the needy was not impulsive, but well regulated. In the warmth of argument at a dinner party, the following remark was drawn from him: "I have been Archbishop of Dublin for so many years. I have given away upwards of £50,000 in charity. I have doubtless frequently erred, but there is one thing with which I cannot reproach myself—I never relieved a beggar in the streets. I take care so to administer relief as not to encourage vice, or its mother, idleness."

To the poor of the district in which he resided, Dr. Whately and his wife were steady friends. Every poor woman, irrespective of her creed, had her weekly pension and bag of coal. When he gave away considerable sums of money to relieve deserving persons in temporary difficulties, he sometimes made them sign a document promising to repay the amount whenever able, not to himself, be it noted, but to persons circumstanced like those who had benefited by his bounty.

From the first year of his episcopate to the last, he dispensed, for the most part secretly, in charity, almost incredible sums. He was thus an example to the rich in his diocese for plainness of living, and ready distribution of this world's wealth.

Dr. Augustus Jessopp, who must be credited to Norfolk, was not so much an eccentric as an individualist. He used to declare that his principal hobbies were "visiting his parishioners, grumbling at the weather, cultivating apples and potatoes, and driving an old horse as far as he'll go". He also said he did not think he would be able to have a gravestone at all. "Things are so bad all round me, and I'm not sure that I shall leave enough to provide decent burial for myself."

After Dr. M. R. James discovered, in an old parochial library at Brent Eleigh, Suffolk, the unique *MS* of the life and miracles of St. William of Norwich, written by Thomas of Monmouth, a Norwich monk, in the twelfth century, he collaborated with the finder in translating it from the Latin.

In his own words when writing to Lady Dorothy Nevill:

> I have been working night and day at St. William of Norwich, the boy saint whom—as fable reporteth it or as liars relate—the Jews of Norwich murdered in A.D. 1144. The Manuscript life of the saint disappeared for more than four centuries, and was fished up in an obscure Suffolk village two or three years ago.

It was published in 1896 in a handsome volume by the Cambridge University Press.

Dr. Jessopp, while staying at Mannington, declared he saw the ghost of Henry Walpole. He was rector of Scarning, near East Dereham from 1879 to 1911.

A. J. Swinburne, in his *Memories of a School Inspector*, has a good deal to say about the parsons and people whom he met when carrying out his duties. He quotes some lines he saw on a vicarage staircase that are somewhat reminiscent of the tea-tray:

> Downward, ever downwards falls the slope of sin,
> Stopping isn't easy, therefore don't begin.

He tells also of a small parish where the choir consisted of a barrel-organ, limited as to its number of tunes, the squealing of a solitary child and the bellow of a young labourer. The congregation consisted of twelve people, and the preacher was usually a locum. One of the worst of the latter brought tears to the eyes of his hearers by a sermon he preached on the triple test of true discipleship, namely, self-surrender, self-sacrifice and self-control, beseeching them to quit the comfortable brotherhood of the indifferent and practise what he preached. During the ensuing week he was carried home in a wheelbarrow from the village inn.

The vicar of this parish, when at home, preached in jerky sentences that ran into one another, with this sort of result:

> We—buried—here
> Mrs. Jones—last week
> Mrs. Thomas—the—week—before
> A—baby—before—that
> Was—carried—to—his
> Eternal—Home
> By—BronchITIS
> And—with—the—wear—and—tear
> Of—the—modern—rush
> Who—knows
> Whose—turn—next?

This was supplemented with:

> The—winter—is—gone
> The—birds—are—singing
> We—Protestants—are—the—birds
> And—with—Christian—joy
> At—the—thought—of— death
> We'll—not—chatter—like—sparrows
> Nor—chirrup—like—sparrows
> But—we'll—warble—like—nightingales.

He further tells of a certain rector who, after a thrilling and tragic story of the fate of two young men who had both slept in damp beds, ushered him into a bedroom one cold night, where his breath produced a mist. "No one has slept in this room", he told Mr. Swinburne cheerily, "for three months—but its much longer than that since any one slept in the other spare room where we've put my wife's mother."

And finally:

At one house we sat down to dinner with one pigeon for five; and before I had recovered from the shock, I found myself politely asked to carve—a most ingenious way out of the difficulty—and would I give the first helping to a mother-in-law upstairs. I have a dazed recollection of a leg coming back to me after I had sent it round, and my feelings then must have been something like those of the five thousand when the miracle had been performed.

In 1851 the Rev. John Mitford, then vicar of Benhall, near Saxmundham, went up to the Great Exhibition. (Some of our old grandfathers walked there and back from that very area.) On his return he told his parishioners that, although everything in the world was said to be there, there was one thing they hadn't got, but which he had in his glebe, a thatched snowstack. This was an enormous heap of snow which he had collected and had had thatched. It lasted from Christmas to Michaelmas as a sort of ice house.

In 1892 the Suffolk papers announced the suicide of a Suffolk clergyman. The account stated: "The inhabitants of the quiet village of Tuddenham St. Martin, near Ipswich, were filled with consternation on Friday afternoon by the report that their esteemed vicar, the Rev. John Pickford, had committed suicide in the grounds of the vicarage."

It appeared that Pickford was unmarried and lived with his sister as housekeeper and his aged mother. He had been an oriental scholar, when that branch of learning first originated (curiously enough from our own Suffolk) and a professor of Sanscrit at Madras. During the twelve years at Tuddenham, he took in Siamese students, presumably to augment a rather poor living. The previous year he had a bad attack of influenza, from which he had suffered much physical and mental distress.

Evidence at the inquest was at a difficulty to discover the reason for his determined suicide. The constable described the manner and method used, viz. a self-inflicted gun-shot wound, and ended with the words: "His ways were strange and I was not much surprised when I heard of it."

The surgeon's evidence came next. He told of the after effects of the influenza, how the deceased had suffered from sleeplessness. He stated that Pickford was a very clever man, had held valuable appointments which he had been obliged to give up through his brain not being able to bear the strain. He went on to say that only the previous Saturday the deceased had come to him suffering from a burnt mouth and could hardly speak. He had taken a large dose of ammonia which had made him sick. The doctor had actually accused him of an attempt at suicide, but Pickford denied it. And so he might have passed, the victim of a mind diseased.

In 1955, Maurice Browne produced a book, *Too Late to Lament*, based on the life story of this unfortunate village clergyman. He was the son of Pickford's friend, the Rev. F. H. Browne, headmaster of Ipswich School. The young Browne found it hard to understand why his father liked 'Horrid Old Pickford', as he became known. This arose from his appearance. He was described as a cross ancient beast, who smelt like a scullery, with dirty clothes slobbered over by grease spots, and with dandruff on his coat collar, scuttling away if a small boy came anywhere near him.

But Browne's father endeavoured to enlighten his son:

Pickford's sister kept house for him in the little village where he was rector, a few miles outside Ipswich; a dour, bitter, selfish woman whom no one liked. So for his sister's sake, he had . . . taken that obscure living in a poky village in a backward county, to make her a home where few could hate her.

One day a letter came addressed to Mr. Pickford. Through several weeks he had been hoping for it; if it came it might offer him an academic position, where he could carry to fruition his life's work in Sanskrit. Every morning his sister went downstairs to meet the postman and see whether the letter had come. "No, John, it has not come to-day; perhaps it will come tomorrow."

Long afterwards the Vice-Chancellor, in whose gift the position lay, meeting Mr. Pickford accidentally in the streets of Ipswich,

greeted him coldly, "I consider it discourteous of you not even to
have acknowledged the offer I made you." Mr. Pickford made no
comment, but when he got back to the ugly lonely village rectory
he spoke to his sister. "Yes", she said defiantly, "of course the
letter came. I read it and burned it. I'm very happy where I am
and you're much better off in a place suited to you."

(I am indebted for the above details to Norman Scarfe's
article in the East Anglian Magazine for June 1963.)

Lady Login, in her *Recollections*, has a good deal to say about
old Felixstowe church. She says:

The then vicar of Walton-cum-Felixstowe felt no qualms at
reducing the ministrations in his cure of souls, which embraced a
district covering nine square miles, to the lowest compatible with
legal requirements. He had four churches to serve, including a
mission chapel at Bawdsey Ferry and the chapel for the garrison at
Landguard Fort; for the performance of which duty he drew pay
as Chaplain from the War Office and thus was enabled to keep a
second curate at seventy pounds a year.

His assistants were never allowed to know until the last moment
—often not until the Sunday morning itself—whether the sermon
would be preached to soldiers, fishermen and coastguards, farmers
and farm labourers, or a congregation of London visitors. As for
himself, he had a certain number of sermons that were taken in
strict rotation, so that hearers knew them as well as he did
himself.

Short and pithy texts were his strong point, and he had a curious
twitch of the nostrils when he wished to be impressive which gave
him the appearance of an old buck rabbit. In those days (1870s),
they had an old three-decker pulpit and box pews. On one occasion he excelled himself. It was a hot summer Sunday and the
church was packed: the children ranged on forms were being
prodded by the beadle, who was rather short-sighted. The barrel
organ had played all its tunes and the bell had gone on ringing
until long past service time, but there was no vicar. Presently he
was seen with his ramshackle pony carriage, lashing the unfortunate white pony into the semblance of a gallop. On arrival he
tore into the vestry, and, reappearing breathlessly hurried through
the morning service. When he came to the sermon, he made his
customary little pause before giving out his text which was "Fear
not, little flock!" repeating the words a second time. He continued: "Before commencing the considering of these words, I
would like to offer some apology for inconvenience caused . . . er

. . . er . . . delay in arriving . . . er . . . er . . . quite a misunder-
standing . . . er." Continuing in the same breath, and with no
change of voice: "These beautiful words will be found written in
the twelfth chapter of St. Luke's Gospel and the thirty-second
verse." His congregation suddenly suffered from colds in the head.
Owing to contradictory instructions, both his curates and himself
had all three turned up to take duty at Landguard Fort.

Colonel Tomline, the chief local landowner, had a violent
antipathy to the Rev. J. H. Maunder, the vicar in question, and
would never give him any assistance. On the other hand he took
a liking to the rector of Trimley St. Mary, who was a great contrast to Maunder. He was a bachelor, sporting in his tastes and
somewhat of a dandy. He drove about in a tilbury (a kind of gig
for two, said to have been so named from its first designer and
maker), sometimes tandem, holding the reins very neatly and
wearing always lavender kid gloves, with a flower in his button-
hole; indeed his turnout was recognizable from a distance. It
would seem as though Tomline was sorry for him, as he was
brother to Palmer the poisoner and had had the courage to keep
to his surname when all the other members of the family changed
it for another.

Mr. Palmer, as the sporting parson, was seldom seen in
clerical attire. His surplice was a very short one, worn without
any cassock, over hunting boots with spurs. He was so dressed
when a new piece of land added to the churchyard was dedicated. He cut a peculiar figure when the Archdeacon and clergy
headed by a choir perambulated the enclosure, striding over the
graves and hopping across rough hummocks of ground.

But the best specimen of all in the eccentric line, was the Rev.
Allot Tighe-Gregory, who was appointed vicar of Bawdsey in
1845 by the Bishop of Norwich, Dr. Stanley. The Bishop declared that Bawdsey was the most neglected parish in his diocese.
Tighe-Gregory held the living for sixty-five years, becoming the
oldest practising priest in the diocese. True, he lived to be a
thorn in the side of a later bishop, as also to the family at the
self-styled Bawdsey Manor. But with all his theatrical manner,
and his black preaching gloves, he did a considerable amount of
good in the village. When he died they said he had christened
more than half of those who formed his congregation, married
many and had buried relatives of nearly all of them.

He established the village school, presumably about 1853, organized a reading room and a lending library, instituted week-night lectures on general subjects, rebuilt the parsonage and restored and maintained the fabric of his church for fifty years at his own expense, his parishioners being but poor farm workers. He also attracted large congregations, particularly so when preaching on 'subjects of the day'. He was something of a musician, could sing a full choral service and composed the words and tune of at least one hymn: "Jerusalem the glorious".

He had three wives but no children. The inscription to his first wife was characteristic, reminding the local inhabitants of her rich and glorious Irish ancestry. That to the second called forth a good deal of interest. It is on a simple stone under the trees:

> Margaret Tighe-Gregory (née Garrod), wife of the vicar of Bawdsey. By birth 'low' as the blessed Virgin. By Intelligence, Education, Marriage, 'Raised' in the estimation of Society. By every Womanly Grace and every Christian Virtue "little lower than the angels". By Death with God. Rev. III.4. Aged 35, April 8, 1877.

She had evidently been maid to his first wife. But surely only an Irishman could write such an epitaph.

For many years, especially latterly, he was looked upon as a joke, and an Irish joke at that. He trained his last two wives to read and write and play the harmonium in church; and was alleged to have kept his coffin under his bed. Physically, he was nothing but skin and bone, and in lieu of an overcoat he wore a large blanket, pinned at his neck with a hugh brooch. When he learned to ride a bicycle at the age of 80, the villagers delighted to watch him pass by, sweeping along from side to side of the road in an endeavour to keep an even keel. Although of such a spare frame and frail in appearance, yet neither accident nor illness could keep him from his work. He was appointed curate at the neighbouring parish of Ramsholt, late in life, hence the bicycle.

There was an old custom religiously kept up in the village, viz. a bonfire on Bonfire Night, the very night the church was burned down. It was customary also to make a guy. Needless to say that on one occasion the guy looked uncommonly like the vicar. How they laughed as he caught fire at every point, his thin face trailing off in wind-swept flames. Whereas at Pakefield they buried their one poor parson alive, here they burned him (in effigy).

6

SUFFOLK VILLAGE

·· ⚱ ··

Nor rural sights alone, but rural sounds,
Exhilarate the spirit, and restore
The tone of languid Nature.

Old Robert Reyce in his Suffolk Breviary hits the mark: "When I consider the degrees and severall callinges of our country inhabitants I thinke it fitt to begin with the poorer sort, from whom all other sorts of estates due take their beginnings."

If we contemplate this village scene of long ago, which happily remains much the same today, the reference to the poorer sort is most apt, for there wasn't a rich man amongst them. That was certainly the case when I was taken to Middleton-cum-Fordley in my mother's arms, all those many years ago. Why? Because for some curious reason, Middleton never possessed a squire of its own; it was a sort of extra-parochial village where all the men were free. That, of course, did not make them that much the more boorish, for I am sure that my grandfather would have touched his cap to the squire regnant of the next village and not account himself that much the more menial. You see, although he didn't know it, grandfather also came of armigerous stock, therefore he was but hailing one of his own peers.

But let us look more closely at this corner of a Suffolk village. If you are a stranger you would no doubt conclude that it is the most uninteresting place you ever saw. You would be within your rights from your limited knowledge, but I am going to suggest to you that you are wrong; for the most interesting parts of the scene are what you can't see, and yet they are all there. For example, the picture (p. 48) may convey something of its peace and serenity, but it cannot indicate the sense of freshness, the

smells, the light and an air so pure and clean that it transmitted
every bit of fragrance from wallflowers to farmyard odours.

> Far from the madding crowd's ignoble strife,
>   Their sober wishes never learn'd to stray;
> Along the cool sequester'd vale of life
>   They kept the even tenor of their way.

To the right is the age-old church, with its delicate little spire,
that even in these years of long ago was denuded of its golden
cockerel, although that fiery bird was probably lying in one of
the outhouses of the rectory. But that noble tower, rearing itself
above the housen, stands for the 'good life' that came to Suffolk
almost as soon as to Canterbury. Within is an ancient ring of
bells that gave out a delightful ting-tang each Sabbath morning.

> Upon a Sabbath-day it fell;
> Twice holy was the Sabbath bell,
>   That call'd the folks to evening prayer.

If you go into the churchyard by the path as indicated, almost
the first gravestone that will meet your gaze is to a Betsy Backhouse. That suggests to me so much of happy things, for Betsy is
a pretty name, and the 'backhouse' was where the brick-oven
lived that provided such lovely tasty bits to help fill a hungry
void. However, the Backhouses lived in an equally beautiful
spot, to wit, the Garden-House Farm on the turnpike.

Betsy, by the way, was a Tabitha Twichet sort of woman, who
wore a multitude of petticoats, and when Mr. Hamilton, the
rector, exhorted her to remember the blessings granted to her in
old age, she replied, "Ah, sir, tew be sure, but they ha' bin taken
out o' me in corns!"

The square-faced building at the end of the row is the chapel,
with a regular old red cap for a roof. This was a place of some
importance, and announces the year of its birth in a little white
stone set plumb in the middle. It has been noted for 'whooly'
good singing, variable preaching, long prayers and much individuality. And not least, wonderful good tea meetings, at which
you could get home-made bread, Bessy Stannard's butter,
Suffolk rusks and a wonderful good cup of tea, dished up in nice
little sprigged cups that were part of its religious vessels.

Now we come to the white-faced building, which was for

6

many a year Joe Broom's shop and the first ever post office. What that meant to the village in social service no tongue can tell. There you traipsed from across the fields, come wind come weather, for a pennorth o' this or that, a little gossip or a bottle of medicine. You opened the door, which immediately set in motion a tingling bell, that kept on tingling until Mister Broom met you with what portion of his shining face his beard had left uncovered. He was a regular old radical was Broom, yet he would touch his cap to the squire, although he was not so handy with the Rector.

But that was not all. On a Whit Monday, that little old shop would break out and erect a stall on that 'three-square' green, near the pump, staffed by his 'gals', who had new print dresses for the occasion. One of the chief items of attraction were rows and rows of saucers of stewed prunes, at a halfpenny a time. There were enough to last from dawn to dusk on a happy day.

Between the chapel and the shop the road goes on and on, past the pretty little rectory and so to the sea, where Dunwich lies fathoms deep in all its magic and mystery.

And there is one thing more, in the picture, yet not in it, because it is etched in shadow. Just to the right of the little twin-gabled cottages, is the village smithy, and that is the travise (a smith's shoeing shed) where Robert Foulsham shoed the 'hosses', made his anvil ring and the sparks fly. If your case was desperate, you could go there and have your teeth 'took out'. "My heart, he was whooly rough." Then off stage, out of the way in the left-hand corner is 'The Bell'. But I mustn't worry you about 'The Bell', save to say it was thatched, smelt of and sold good beer, and was too often patronised by Joe Broom's two sons.

One other thing. Not one of those little houses that you can see, and all those you can't see, but contained bits and pieces you will find today in antique shops and museums. They were then thought little of, save "that belonged to my poor old mother, and that's as old as old can be".

However, with all this I have left out the ghosts of those who lived behind those railings on the left in the picture, and those of the Barhams, Baldrys, Fisks, Larters, Mayhews, Newsons, Rouses and Spalls, who shuffled along that village street, to church, chapel, shop or 'Bell'.

Peace, Peace! such a small lamp illumes, on this highway
  So dimly, so few steps in front of my feet—
Yet shows me that *their* way is parted from my way
  Out of sight, beyond light, at what goal may we meet?

7

MIDDLETON MOOR
AND THE MEETINERS

That our ancient Liturgy may be restored,
That the organs (by Sectaries so much abhorred),
May sound divine praises according to the word,
Te rogamus audi nos.

The Old Protestant Litany, 1647.

In old Suffolk parlance Middleton Moor would be described as
a 'three-square' green, otherwise known as triangular. It is on
the West side of the turnpike as one goes from Yoxford to Leiston, and is separated from the rest of the village by Hulver Hill,
which is an old word for holly; and by the Carnser, which is
another old word for a causeway or raised footpath between two
dykes. Here, naturally enough, you will find Causeway Farm.
In fact the whole district is studded with ancient lovely names,
little bits of byroads; and memories enough to cover the web of
years since the Saxons made this their home.

Middleton is really made up of two ancient parishes. Its full
designation is Middleton-cum-Fordley; and whether the moor
is in Middleton or Fordley I am not positive to say. Because if
you take the little winding way on the east side of the turnpike,
you come smack on to Fordley Hall, which is, perhaps, the
oldest house in the parish. But of this I am not quite sure, for
Moor Farm on the north side of the green is about the same age.
It stands there with its lovely gable-end of old red brick, a verit-
able triumph of the builder's art; while inside, in what was the
parlour chamber, is one of the best examples of a pargeted
overmantel that you will find anywhere.

Now you will gather from this that the moor has a long history. At one time, even from time out of mind, the villagers had

84

the right to keep geese on the green. They gaggled about together, keeping to their own families and relations, as geese do, and thereby provided the traditional dish for old Michaelmas Day—and the best feather beds and pillows for miles around.

I should mention in passing that this keeping of geese did not make the folks hereabouts any more "gawmless" (silly, heedless), than the other villagers. It's true they called the parish cage or lock-up, the "goose-house"; but geese, as far as my observation goes, are not half as stupid as chickens, or sheep for that matter. It was seldom, if ever, that they got "runned" over, or drowned and became, like certain "owd yows" when crossing a ditch, "jump short" mutton.

Which brings to mind the tale about old Betsy Backhouse (mother of Philemon Charles, who kept the Garden House farm), who purported to be a "Groper", and who suffered from "vaserlated" (ulcerated), legs.

This, by the way, was an ancient secret gift, bestowed on at least one old woman in a village, enabling her by certain gropings with her fingers to tell if a goose or duck was impregnated. Betsy's reputation at such a practice remained secure until certain vulgar "bors" of the baser sort palmed off a gander on to her; and she didn't notice it. But then she was getting towards her "arternune".

I should have told you that the moor is uneven in its surface, for it has a number of hollows, formed possibly by digging for sand. Naturally enough, in wet weather these become ponds; but, unlike the pond under the willows at Yankee Farm, which stands by the lane to Fordley Hall, they dry up almost as rapidly as they fill. To these grassy hollows the gipsies came, season by season, hobbled their horses, parked their painted wagons, and opened their umbrella tents. They were welcomed, partly because they were known, partly because of their knowledge and love of horseflesh and partly because they bore about them the aura of mystery, the mystery of over the hills and far away. That was indeed an unknown country to those whose furthest knowledge was the market town or Southwold Fair. One of these Romanys was an acceptable preacher at Middleton chapel:

Round was his face and "camois" [hooked] was his nose. And he would take as his text: "Noe was a just man and a parfit."

Then too, in these green hollows which acted as a natural

arena, prize-fights were held, the contestants always coming from a distance. They would set to and were 'whooly gored up' before they finished, watched among others by certain local squires.

But perhaps the strangest occasion of all, was when an open-air baptism took place in February 1908, for four males and two females. It was bitterly cold weather, as well it might be, for the hollows only filled up in winter. But this did not deter those who had set their mind on this profession of faith. They were duly dipped in ice-cold water in pouring rain. Somehow or other they managed to make picture post cards of the scene, so great was the novelty.

Now the very date is interesting, in that it is so far away and long ago, when the countryside was wrapped in peace. Before Armageddon came and contentment vanished; and before the burning Zeppelin blazed in a fearful doom over nearby Theberton.

Naturally enough the news got round and tongues began to wag. Who were these "pogramites" [Suffolk for dissenters]? "They were them owd Mormons," said some; others called them "dippers" and left it at that.

It appeared that the instigators were two women, dressed in black with little black hats, who had hired a cottage in Brook Street, Yoxford. They were members of a No Sect (which sounds something of an anachronism even for old Suffolk), held meetings there and in the open-air, and tramped the neighbourhood as in ancient days the friars must have done from the ruined abbeys thereabouts. And they made converts. The open-air baptism was the crowning point of their labours; before which, be it noted, a long open-air service had taken place in the stingy weather of a February fill-dyke, and another similar service afterwards. So much for an exhibition of endurance.

It might be mentioned of these, who still exist as a small community, that they have the reputation of being thoroughly good people. They have no meeting places save their own homes, do considerable missionary work and live as near to the primitive Christians as is possible. Their chief distinguishing feature of dress seems to be black stockings for the women and black socks for the men. And, as with certain other professors of a simple religion, a closeness in relationship between the members.

Meetiners have always enjoyed a certain freedom in Suffolk; and a sturdy independence of view has characterised its folk, as Cromwell discovered. Chapels were almost as numerous as the "chuches", and *Pilgrim's Progress* was held in as much esteem as the Bible itself. It even passed into common speech when an old rabbit catcher could put in another ferret after one that had lain up, with: "Gew yew in Pilgrim an' sarch out Progress!" And they were prepared to endure hardship for the cause, as the old woman who would lock up her cottage and walk seven miles to the meeting and seven miles back every Sabbath. And be rarely vexed and put out if she couldn't do it.

Curiously enough, Primitive Methodists were described as "ranters", presumably because they ranted. Now this was a word well known in this part of Suffolk, for it was applied to a large tin or copper can in which the beer was brought from the cellar and poured into drinking vessels. "Pass the ranter!" was the familiar cry in the harvest field when the time came to partake of the beer specially brewed for the exhausting labours of that season. In drinking the men would never drain the mug, but cast a little on the ground; which was but another sign of a religious influence which dominated their lives and their work.

8

A SUFFOLK FARMHOUSE

········

When I was a little boy and came down to Suffolk with my mother from grimy London, houses like the one illustrated facing page 48 were quite common, and almost every village had at least one. Some had fallen in the world and been chopped up to form a two-dweller, but most were still farmhouses, albeit lived in by the bailiff rather than the farmer. How pleasantly they stood, thatched or tiled, habitations of long ago, where men had lived and loved, toiled and died. On the central chimney stack would be a date, evocative of Spanish Armadas and days and years of that most illustrious princess, *Elizabetha Magna Regina Angliae.*

Some were L-shaped, but they invariably presented a front similar to this Old Hall Farm, which so happily still survives, but "whooly growed up" in the world. The porch, with its tiny bedroom above, had followed the pattern of the old Halls, once with open ceilings to the roof, as in a church or barn. The front would be creeper hung, where birds nested and insects flourished; or it might be jasmine, spangled over with butterflies and humming bees. And there were the sentinel trees at each end; why, I do not know, but always there. Perhaps a plum or a pear worth the eating, or a couple of trembling aspens, in which the wind made strange noises, reminding one small person of the Lord God speaking to Adam and Eve. After all, the trees were in a tiny garden, so what more appropriate than such a thought.

But the plot was not complete without the encircling wall. This might be of brick, rubble or the local flints; but always capped with a rounded top, made I have no doubt in some local brick kiln, otherwise known as a kell. In the case of this Old

Hall Farm the wall is of particular interest, composed as it is of bits of dressed stone-work that must have come from the Old Hall itself across the fields, used by Edward III as a kicking-off place for Crecy. You didn't go to a builders' merchant in those far off days, you took something near at hand that cost "nawthin". And what a nice little, delicate bit of carpentering went to the making of the wicket gate!

Now I "kinder" reckon that must have bin a bit of a scorcher when this photograph was taken, because the windows and door are open. Perhaps the "fooks" had gone "fair modern".

You must further know that a house of this description was also a business premises. This is evident by the door and window on the right, which was the dairy. Of course, usually over a dairy window you had a rowan tree to ward off evil influences exercised by witches. But I don't think this is the case here. Perhaps it is only a plum, which gives rise to the couplet:

> The higher the plum tree the riper the plum:
> The richer the cobbler, the blacker his thumb.

But there is one other feature of this lovely old house to which I would draw your attention, and that is the chimney stack at the gable end, with its inconsequential bit of a chimney pot. Why chimney pot? We shall never know. However, this much I can tell you, it belongs to the backhouse and the backhouse was something to be reckoned with. If the little wall in front was a sort of fortification, the backhouse at the rear was equally protected, because it was guarded by a half-hatch door. This not only kept out the "owd hins" and geese, but also unwanted callers. Such for instance as Polly Vincent (pronounced with a W), who, as grandmother wrote to her gals up in London, "Yew know how she do wheedle hare way in. If she git as much as a little finger in yar place, it bain't long afore the rest on her follows. But that bean't exactly how she goo out."

Here also dwelt the backhouse boy. Now backhouse boys might be deaf and dumb, but they might be quite otherwise, voluble and aged. For example, one had an immense tongue, and when the empty plates came in from the high table, he emulated the Prodigal Son and dished the pigs of part of their swill by licking them clean, including any gooseberry shucks or other tasty leavings. And there was the one who complained righteously enough about his lot: "I reckon thass a regular masterpiece. Yow wark all noight for one-and-six a day, an' then yew git nuffin. Well, I call that suffen!"

The backhouse was where all the work was done. There stood the great brick oven and the copper, and perhaps a pump. It was the hub of the house where all the culinary work was carried out, not forgetting the ham pickling, the pounding of sugar and spice in a mortar and the carefully-watched, spiced beer seething on the hob.

Of the house proper, the room on the left of the porch was the keeping room, so named because it was kept for special occasions. Here could be found in solemn splendour Staffordshire figures, coloured prints, straw-work boxes, old glass tumblers that rang like bells, willow-pattern china, pewter and brass. To say nothing of a bit or two of Sheraton or Chippendale. There might even be a pair of shells on the mantelpiece.

> The Ocean scarce spoke louder with his swell
> Than breathes the mimic murmurer in the shell.

The upper rooms were of considerable interest. You climbed up a little staircase and found yourself plump in the best bedroom; and all the other rooms led out from one another, there being no passages. Neither were all the rooms on one level, you stepped down or up as you crossed the threshold. The floors sagged as they had settled, and their wide chestnut boards shone with many applications of elbow grease and beeswax, while the blacksmith-made nails lined themselves up like studs in a suit of armour.

In the best bedroom would be a four-poster, in some cases a real gem, out from Chippendale's workshop. These beds were the pride and joy of the farmer's wife and a complete luxury added to a full life. Sometimes, as in the case of grandfather, the goodman snored, developing into a determined rip-snorter. But grandmother was equal to this. Unbeknown to grandfather, she sewed a cotton reel into the middle of the back of his nightshirt. And somehow that fair cured him.

Usually the bedroom walls were whitewashed, but when wallpaper became a bit more common, the rooms were enlivened by sundry stripes and bunches of flowers. One enterprising owd gal managed to get hold of a couple of those large pattern books,

and she knew what to do with them. She set to work, cut the
loose sheets lozenge-shape, and there was enough to cover the
whole room, patchwork quilt-like. That was a masterpiece.

But there, as Yeats has expressed it:

> The innocent and the beautiful
> Have no enemy but time.

Alas, the ethos of these old farmhouses has departed, with the
poppy-laden fields of Suffolk, the stooks in the harvest field, the
stacks in the stackyard, and the halloo of the "hold-yer" boy.

> The auld wife sat at her ivied door,
> (Butter and eggs and a pound of cheese)
> A thing she had frequently done before;
> And her spectacles lay on her apron'd knees.
>
> The farmer's daughter hath soft brown hair;
> (Butter and eggs and a pound of cheese)
> And I met with a ballad, I can't say where,
> Which wholly consisted of lines like these.

9

GRANDFATHER'S CHAIR

··◦✧◦··

As the goodman saith, so say we;
But as the goodwife saith, so must it be.

Grandmother may have been a poor frail woman, with long veinous hands and a pale face, who always wore a lace cap and a shawl and was right scrabbed with the cold; yet it was mutually agreed in the house that she was boss. Besides, she was reputed to grow the finest stocks in her bit of garden. However, if all she surveyed in backhouse, kitchen-parlour, and the chambers above were her domain, one thing was not hers, and that was grandfather's chair. Of course, she had a chair of her own, but it was less cosy, more upright, to allow her to work with her needle, and had a footstool, an adjunct almost by divine right. A chair has been described as a seat of authority, but it did not apply in grandfather's case. Suffice it to say it was his chair.

Grandfather's chair was Georgian, with lovely curving lines, that seemed to speak comfort and rest, and was covered in turkey-twill that was such a protective colour. Broom found it a splendid saleable article in his general shop, contrasting finely with his roll of grey flannel. It was the very same shade that provided the old women with their flannel petticoats; stays for the children, including the little boys; and neckerchiefs for the men, so much in evidence in the harvest field. Besides, it was a colour not approved of by witches, hence the rowan trees to be found near an old house; and grandmother even used it for the little curtain drawn across her brick-oven door to keep the devil or the fairies from interfering with her weekly bake.

Of course, there were other chairs in grandmother's home. I

remember them so well, all as old as old could be; in some cases polished smooth by many persons sitting there; in others, like her turned-ash chairs in her backhouse, painted green. Just think, they formed one of the three essentials of a home, a bed, a table, a chair. For many a long year they were largely supplied by the wood-turner, so that in the *Turner's Ordinance* of 1478, they are included with, "Shovells, scoops, bushell trees, washing bowls, wheels, pails, trays, truggers wares, and wooden measures." But by 1604 chair-making had become the province of the joiner.

In Wheatley's *Cries of London*. 'Old Chairs to Mend', 1795, re-rushing a chair-bottom, shows a common type of ladder-back chair, often to be found in farmhouses, cottages and kitchens. Rushes abounded in grandfather's marshy district, and he knew how to use them. This sort of industry may well have given rise to the old Suffolk saying: "Go to Bungay to get new bottomed." Bungay, after all, was within jogging distance of grandfather's home. Of one thing I am quite sure, that there were chair-makers at Halesworth and probably other market towns nearby. And there were those glorious creations of the old wheelwright, Daniel Day, and his son Richard at Mendlesham.

Grandfather's chair was his one great daytime luxury, his night solace being the feather bed on the old four-poster. But that, of course, was shared. He would sit four-square within its curving wings and arms, bolt upright, his hands cupped on his thighs, appearing almost ashamed since they had nothing to do. He was possibly thinking of his work, whether he should call in the vet to see Blossom, or whether those young pigs should be "ringled". Or if "Spade" Newson and "Earnie-can-dig" Wool-nough had completed the draining of the "ten acre"? He may even have had a thought to his gun in the corner, or how he must clean those old casks ready for next week's brew. He might even have been reading his Bible, a huge family affair, which had been presented to him by the rector, although he was a Methodist. Reading was not one of his great accomplishments, but he liked the story about Jacob and Rachael and could picture the scene with all those sheep needing a watering. As the old book had large print, he could finger his way along. All the same, he thought Jacob was a crafty grab-all, and he wouldn't have cared for him as a "nabor".

Grandmother's chair was one of those beautiful creations from Mendlesham out of her own country. These chairs, mostly with arms, very few being known without, were made in a wheelwright's yard. Sheraton, who, Herbert Cescinsky once said, "was probably the greatest educator of our eighteenth-century cabinet makers", certainly had a hand in its lovely delicate back, even if it did come out of a Suffolk village. The splats and a little stringing inlay enlivened and enriched the whole. The turning of the legs and stretchers, as also the spindles in the back, suggested the pole-lathe, while the fretted baluster, the delightfully smooth-shaped arms and supports with their almost volute endings, added charm to the whole and completed a craftsmanly production, even though the seat was a solid piece of elm, adzed to shape. How it gleamed and shone under its constant rubbing.

The possession of such, now treasured, belongings might suggest that my grandparents' cottage home was elegantly furnished. But such was not the case; it was comfortably characteristic of those years before the despoiler came to the backhouse door in search of 'antiques'. The stuff would have been acquired by means of an auction, that village festival, where one could come by so much for a shilling or eighteenpence. In those far off days heirlooms were valued because they had belonged to others, which extended to the things of everyday use, even the brewing utensils. They were that much better for having been tested and tried. Besides, of course, beer tasted better for having been brewed by old brown handcups, funnels and tubs.

Yes, grandfather's chair figured in the auction when his dear old home was dispersed. How much it fetched I can't remember, but I do know it went to an old artist who lived in an Elizabethan farmhouse with an Italianate addition at the back; certainly a curious combination.

I loved that old comfortable chair, because once as a little boy on a visit to Elysium from our London suburban home I fell asleep in it. A most unusual occurrence, because there was so much to love and do and smell in that peaceful world of yesterday, deep-set in a Suffolk countryside.

GRANDFATHER'S COAT OF ARMS

Fresh spring the herald of love's mighty king,
In whose coat armour richly are display'd
All sorts of flowers the which on earth do spring
In goodly colours gloriously array'd.

Spencer.

He that loves the tree loves the branch

Believe it or not, but grandfather belonged to an armigerous family and was entitled to wear a coat of arms. If you are incredulous you can find it tricked out in a little parchment-covered volume, twelve inches by seven-and-threequarter inches and half an inch thick, entitled, *The Arms of All the Autient Families in Suffolk*, forming one of four such volumes, known as the "Blois MSS" and deposited in the Record Office at Ipswich. The arms are thus described: "Argent on a fesse Gules, between 3 beares Sable tired Gold [that is with gold muzzles or chains], a fleur de lis enclosed by two martlets of the field." Crest: "A stork among bullrushes, all proper." But no trace of a motto.

The more I think about it, the more I am inclined to laugh, that my poor old thrifty grandparent whom I knew and loved so well, with his horny hands and slouching gait as he moved about the farmyard and the fields, earning as much as eight shillings a week when in full employment, should have been so gloriously endowed. I feel sure he would have been only too ready to join in the laughter, especially if it had been pointed out to him that the three bears were a play on his name and not something out of a story book for children. He was main fond of

a joke. His bucolic countenance would have glowed with merri-
ment as he exclaimed: "Well, thare, partner, what dew yew
think on't, thet'll whooly staam yew!" Alas, he never knew, or
he might have given voice to the old aphorism: "It is good
sheltering under an old hedge." His career was better described
by the philosophic lines:

> The villager, born humbly and bred hard . . .
> Enjoys more comforts in a single hour
> Than ages give the wretch condemn'd to power.

It would certainly have been a strange sight for a hatchment
to have been hung up outside his cottage home or on the walls
of his Methodist chapel when he died.

It is all very well for those who write on heraldry to warn us
seekers after aggrandisement that people of the same name are
not necessarily related to one another. But if your name was
Barham and you lived in days when movement was restricted
to a few miles, twenty at most, and were quite unlike the
"borealis race of travellers that flit ere you can point the place",
and you lived in the next village to where a Suffolk branch of
the family was located, you might reasonably assume that you
were of that kindred. There a Barham married a Hatcher (a
name still to be found in Middleton, though Barham is not), and
another a daughter of Thomas Etheridge of Veales Hall,
Fressingfield, away back in the seventeenth and eighteenth
centuries. Barham is not that common a name, and although my
grandfather was so poor, as were his neighbours and kindred,
yet his conduct was entirely honourable, and he could hold his
head high. Certainly his fellows spoke well of him, who bore the
font name of John. Besides, one must recall the import of the old
saying, so pertinent in his day: "Fields have eyes and woods
have ears."

Naturally enough, this aura of an ancient and bedizened
family extended to his wife and family, who looked through the
same old Elizabethan windows as he. Grandmother was a
Brown, true she was a brunette whereas the Saxons were blond
(Suffolk people claim that descent), but you can hardly hyphen-
ate that; and it would be difficult to sort out her escutcheon even
if she had had one. Just as she shared his outlook and his life, so
she shared his penury:

A baker's wife may bite of a bun,
A brewer's wife may drink of a tun,
A fishmonger's wife may feed of a conger,
But a servingman's wife may starve for hunger.

Fortunately, through his enterprise and endeavour, grandfather was able to see to it that she didn't starve.

Certainly the blue-bloodedness passed to her daughters, one of whom was my mother, who exhibited in no uncertain manner an independent and upright character. This, in spite of the fact that her introduction to life was contained in the little *vademecum* of village girls at that time, *My Station and its Duties*, a narrative for girls going into service. Here the village schoolmistress instructs her little flock not only on the moral duties of a servant, but implores them not to allow their feet "to smell".

Those who knew Suffolk and its people in the quiet days of yesterday will know that grandfather's case was in no way unique. Many village folk, by implication and inference, were conscious of their kinship with the 'Big House'. They spelt their name in the same way, and were mighty proud of it; and, although they touched their hat to the squire, they knew they were of the same kin.

This recording of pedigrees was the polite accomplishment of our old country parsons, one of whom was so greatly attached to the pursuit that he had the names of the chief gentry around him painted on the windows of his church, until the place fairly glowed with colour. Another, the Rev. Matthias Candler, vicar of Coddenham, accumulated a considerable MSS. Moreover, he was said to be honest withal. That, of course, because one might find uncomfortable incidents in the process. In his case it was a distant cousin who had killed his father and been hanged for it at Bury St. Edmunds. Others might be found to be "not gentlemen of Coat Armour, being yeomen and traders".

These old searchers and collectors of arms, who had nothing else to do, found it an exciting and rewarding pastime, unearthing eccentricities which might otherwise have passed unnoticed. There were the two Alstons of Newton, the one who "was wont allwaies to goe clad in Blew cloth", and the other who had a "very red face". Besides being "slaine in the warres", one unlucky wight was "blone up with gunpowder in a warehouse in Ipswich". Another had five wives and many children,

7

but also a great estate on which to rear them. And of one lady it was recalled that "her second husband had been third husband to her first husband's mother". Which seems to be a record even in a Suffolk countryman's attempt at recounting his family connections.

In grandfather's case the recorder was a Rev. William Tyllotson, curate of Capel, near Hadleigh, in 1594, whose collection was evidently incorporated and re-written by two members of the Blois family, father and son, and now form part of the aforesaid Blois MSS. The seat of that family was, and is, thank God, Cockfield Hall, Yoxford, where the MSS were found in 1809.

Somehow or other I always thought I was somebody, but now I know. Besides, I have coveted the right to wear a signet ring and the bearing of a crest. Alas, the female side does not inherit such things, so my hopes, so nearly realized, are completely shattered. I must take refuge in the old saying: "He that hath no head needs no hat." But it is nice to think that somewhere under the skin runs that old stream, tinct with blue.

Which leads me to ask—have you ever had occasion to look for your grandfather? If so, you will have found the pathway full of adventure. Perhaps you have thought you would like to do so but have never made a start. You may have heard he was related to so-and-so, and it would be nice to be able to confirm it. Really, after all, you never know. Neither need any one else know if he turns out to have been hung for murder. All you do is to turn over the page and stop looking. However, it may prove otherwise, and you will be able to quote the verse feelingly:

> I'll sing you a good old song,
>   Made by a good old pate
> Of a fine old English gentleman
>   Who had an old estate,
> And who kept up his old mansion
>   At a bountiful old rate;
> With a good old porter to relieve
>   The old poor at his gate,
> Like a fine old English gentleman
>   All of the olden time.

Ancestor worship is very old. Whether the Chinese began it I cannot say. Certainly they hung up lanterns at the graves of the departed. After all, they were credited with wisdom when we were savages. Victorians were great at it too, partly because they helped to create the tangled skeins which we do our best to unravel. In those days, the title and the estate and most of the money, went to the heir, who was the eldest son. Younger sons had a thin time of it and a poor look out, in fact they often disappeared into obscurity, joining the army as gentlemen rankers or emigrating. Naturally enough, this sort of thing passed into the sentimental novel and made lovely reading for housemaids. I have just read such a short story in a collection for which I paid fifteen shillings, being led away by the title. (But there, the old tag about a fool and his money still stands.) In this case the hero was an omnibus conductor of the horse-drawn variety, hence the full definition—omnibus.

"Annie," said I, when we had finished our ride, "did you notice that omnibus conductor? I am sure he was a gentleman. His hands were so white and thin, and he spoke so nicely, and had such a refined face. He handed me out of the omnibus with a courtly grace of his own that would have done credit to a duke."

Presently we came to a stopping place. Now, I thought, I'll interview him.
"I believe," said I, coming to the point with startling abruptness. . . . "I believe you are a gentleman."
"No, Madam," he said proudly, "you are mistaken; no gentleman, only a bus conductor."

The story continues, reaching its denouement within a couple of pages:

Although the lady had a pretty victoria and a mare named Madge that was quite frisky at times, she was determined to take another omnibus ride, and probe into this romance: "You are like someone I know, tell me your name."
He hesitated, got very red and then said grumpily enough, "My name is Frank Lockhart, Madam."
And now I knew why the face was familiar to me, for that was the name of the handsome young tutor who beguiled my bonny sister Rose into marrying him, just nineteen years ago. He was my brother's tutor, a gentleman by birth and education, but poor. . . .
"And is your mother living, Frank?" said I, "and may I come and see her?"

"Yes, Madam, she is living, but we are poor people, best by ourselves, and where we lodge is quite unfit for you to visit," continued he, glancing at my costly furs. . . .

Et cetera and et cetera, *ad nauseam*.

If you belong to Suffolk, by which I mean by birth and breeding, you can tell a better tale than that. You may not be able to prove your people came over with Norman William. Possibly you can go one better and say you were here already. However, you will probably have to be content with something a bit later. For if you walk into one of our ancient village churches, you may possibly see on the north or south sides of the sanctuary, a canopied tomb of a knight in armour. If you pursue the subject you will undoubtedly find his name. It will be a local name, perhaps your very own, to be found in the village, borne by the local folks until the Great War, and now, alas, known there no more. This knight may have been a Crusader, or fought at Agincourt or Cressy; a soldier of England and his Suffolk in battles long ago.

But perhaps he is not perpetuated in stone; he may be lying on an alabaster monument, his lady by his side, as the Bardolfs at Dennington. Or he may have a brass, tricked out in full armour, his feet on his favourite hound, his sword by his side, and his head resting on his crested helmet. Sometimes, I wonder, did they strut about their village street, these long-dead knights? Did they come to church fully accoutred? If so, they would have had to remove their visored head-dresses on entering, and in consequence, must have looked like divers, *sans* helmets, their long-haired heads sticking up above their unbending and steely breasts.

This may all sound like a bit of poppy-cock, but it is not so. I once wrote an article for a well-known journal, in which I mentioned the *Household Book of Dame Alice de Bryene*. She lived at Acton in West Suffolk, as a widow, and died 7th March 1435. Her beautiful brass is in the church there. When she married she lived in the West of England, but when her husband died young she came to live amongst her own people for she was the daughter of Sir Robert de Bures. The point is that I soon received a letter with the name of "de Bryene" on the heading, asking me where the writer could obtain a copy of the book.

Among the Lady's employees, whose names appear, are John

Fowler, shepherd; Robert Mose, smith; Richard Bonys, mower; John Colbrook, harvestman; John Skoyl, rent collector, and John White, farmer. (These do not differ largely from the list of servants to be found on a country estate in Victorian times, viz: blacksmith, painter and plumber etc.; carpenter, bricklayer, drainer and estate worker, estate labourer, woodman, carter, farm labourer, gardener, coachman, first and second keeper.)

Sir Robert de Bures, of our Suffolk village, was a crusader, as evidenced by his mail-clad crossed legs on a brass at Acton Church. Which reminds me of that marvellous pavement floor of the pro-cathedral at Valetta, Malta. It is a blaze of colour. I had the good fortune of a guide to myself when I was there, and he informed me he was constantly getting enquiries from families in search of their ancestors, about the coats-of-arms there displayed. And have you ever seen the inns of these same Crusaders at Rhodes?

I have just been looking up my own folks and found the game quite exciting. Let me tell you what happened.

My father was born in 1850, which is a long time ago. I started searching in Somerset House, to discover that their records do not start until 1837. My first find was my father's birth certificate. I imagined it would be quite easy from there, but it wasn't.

I should say that my paternal grandfather, whom I never knew, had a peculiar middle name that distinguished him, but no one knew anything about him; and I let my father die without telling me any details he might have known.

I next discovered that one of the best points from which to start is the 1851 census. This was the first record that gives the place of birth as well as that of residence. So up I went to the Public Record Office in Chancery Lane, to try my luck. I approached a very pleasant-looking official, with an air of great simplicity, telling him I was looking for my grandfather. He glanced at me, noted my white hair, grinned and said he thought my relative must be dead. I assured him he was, at least I had good reason to think so.

When I gave him a few more particulars he was attentiveness itself. He told me to find a seat and that he would bring me that part of the census returns dealing with my particular district. But there was no seat, the room was full of people searching and making notes, copying out from mediaeval manuscripts, all intent on what looked a very dry-as-dust occupation. I noticed there were a lot of coloured men at work, presumably law students in training.

As there were no seats to be had, I discovered that there were counters at the side for standing only. They were fitted with numbers, each number denoting a stance. I took a place at the ready, waiting. It was not long before a very friendly person next to me, a young woman, pointed out a seat that had just become vacant. I suggested she took it, but she advised me to be quick lest someone else got it, so I obeyed. That is the sort of kindness that one meets in those places. I had noticed the same helpfulness in the Reading Room at the British Museum.

My papers duly arrived, in a cardboard box, the contents tied up with tape (not red). The sheets were the original returns that had been copied out from the individual papers, written with a quill pen, in the best copper-plate. They had been classified parish by parish for the whole of the county. I found the writing rather difficult to read, and it was a somewhat wearisome business going up and down the columns. It was certainly a paper chase. I had foolishly imagined that I could have got the information I wanted in a matter of minutes, but it was not so. Up and down the columns I went, but the magic name I was searching for did not appear. Meanwhile the clock ticked on relentlessly, and I had to give it up.

But having set one's face to the plough, it was useless to turn back, although it was some time before I was able to resume the search. Once again I ran into my same smiling friend as before, who greeted me with more laughter. This time I was directed to a seat in the circular room, rather similar to the Reading Room at the British Museum, but much smaller. I discovered that the gentleman next to me was busy on a long parchment, and when he most conveniently disappeared for a few minutes, I took a glance at his work. It was really beautiful, as fine as the original, which was done on a long scroll. I waited longer on this occasion but presently my package appeared and I set to work.

At first it seemed as fruitless as before, a wearisome progress through old forgotten dead, when suddenly I came on familiar ground. It was of people, my relatives that I already knew, so I passed on, conning several pages. Then something induced me to go back, and the very person I was looking for was before me. I had passed my grandfather in the street, but had not recognized him. The only thing was that the middle name, the key to the riddle, was missing, but his birthplace was given. I parcelled up the package and left. Now, thought I, the way is plain, I have found the salt to put on his tail.

Here, I can tell you, the job is not as easy as at first appears, for now I was to come up against clerical stupidity. I wrote to the vicar of the parish, giving him the relevant dates, and asking him if he could trace the entry of birth in the registers. After some days I was told there was no evidence of an entry. And further, that the registers did not start until ten or fifteen years after the date given. He did not tell me that the earlier registers were in the county record office, which he must have known. And, in passing, these parish records do not give the date of birth, only that of baptism; and as there were no laws in operation for compulsory registration, particularly if the person concerned was a Non-Conformist, or the parents did not present the child for baptism, there is no trace.

My next move was to contact the county archives. After some days I received a letter to say the registers were there, that they had been searched, but there was no trace of a baptism for the person concerned. I was up against a dead end. They did not tell me the relevant pages were missing. Evidently some careless or illiterate parson was to blame, or perchance a fire had destroyed the records. I sometimes wonder how folks manage when they come up against these gaps, which are all too numerous, and as far as I can see, insurmountable.

However, the motto of the searcher must always be *nil desperandum*, and I decided to have a day out and visit the town in question and its archives. I regret to say I came up against indifferent assistance. I couldn't help thinking that this sort of thing was in violent contrast to our own Record Office at Ipswich. There they would have fallen over themselves to help, even to unearthing the dear deceased, as I very well knew from experience. After chasing several files and producing nothing, I left with a heavy heart. However, one suggestion was made, that I consulted the local probate office.

Such a feeling of frustration suggested a very nice lunch, which I accomplished, and, after some wanderings, I arrived at the Office. This was of such prominence that an enquiry opposite as to its whereabouts, elicited complete ignorance. Here I came up against more difficulties, the redeeming feature being a young girl who seemed strangely out of place in such ancient surroundings. I tried the same blandishments on her I had used at the Record Office in Chancery Lane, with some success. Dusty volumes were produced, which I soon discovered I could have consulted anywhere. It was with difficulty I managed to obtain a written list of local wills. These were done up in years, and in only the second year was the very gentleman I was searching for. I nearly hailed him with a shout. Not only did I find one, but there were two; my forebear, I discovered, had died young, when only 30 years of age. This find was indeed a triumph.

This chance encounter with my long-dead grandfather, led me into discovering other relations of mine. From the will of my grandfather it was evident he anticipated possible bequests, for the second name belonged to his uncle, a reasonably wealthy man. He died soon after my grandfather, leaving a carriage, horses, wine cellar and what not, but nothing to his nephew, not even a Lincolnshire feather bed. He had daughters but no son, and the girls were married off to clergy with nice little dowries of a £1,000 apiece. So I may be distantly (ah, how distantly) related to the Bench of Bishops, as also to the Faculty of Medicine.

And here is the sequel. That grandfather of mine, so difficult to trace, would have been described as eminently respectable, but as far as I know, could lay no claim to a coat-of-arms. My other grandfather, of honest yeoman stock, a farm labourer, would have touched his hat to the other. Yet he was entitled to a magnificent achievement because he belonged to an old Suffolk family.

First Clown. There is no ancient gentleman but gardener, ditcher, and grave-maker: they hold up Adam's profession.
Second Clown. Was he a gentleman?
First Clown. He was the first that ever bore arms.

GRANDMOTHER'S GARDEN

··❦··

Shall I not one day remember thy bower
One day when all days are one day to me?

Could one ever forget a Suffolk cottage garden of those dear
dead years that are gone? I trow not. It might be a wilderness of
this and that; yellow evening primrose, geranium calceolaria,
phlox, clarksia, stocks, hollyhocks, paeonies and French mari-
golds. But it might be quite otherwise; trim and neat, with
sanded paths and tiny box borders. Yet, one or other, it was,
and is, an unforgettable memory. It was composed of several
ineffable elements: sky, sun and air, colour, perfume; and a
peace that this generation cannot ever know. I was only a tiny
boy when I first saw my grandmother's garden with conscious
eyes, but I have never forgotten that utter loveliness and abiding sanctity. "Ah God, if again it might be."

But then, grandmother's home was worthy of such a garden.
A real Suffolk cottage, set so peacefully under a Suffolk sky. Its
pantile roof was once of thatch, but that was long years ago,
when Suffolk gentlemen had their coats hung in the village
church. (I like the one for the Worthington family, that dear
old Robert Reyce found in the parish church of Preston, near
Lavenham, viz: Argent, three muck forkes sable on a canton
ermin a dexter hand gules. I could aspire no higher.)

The window frames jut out from the wattled front, and the
lower windows and the doors have drip-boards that give them
an attractive eyebrow-like appearance. The door has a Suffolk
latch, and all are painted a glistering white. But I would draw
your attention to that lovely bit of artistry, to wit the down pipe

of zinc, with its pleasant little head, made by some village plumber for the job, leading to the rain-water tub in the corner. And lest you should be misled, the red brick chimney belongs to the backhouse, where all the brewing and the baking, the washing and the pickling was done. I wonder if she ever made that country delicacy of dock-leaf pudding, comprising sweet dock leaves, nettles, hard-boiled eggs and spring onions. Or if grandfather refused to eat it? However, he could have said with Herrick:

> Lord, Thou hast given me a cell
> Wherein to dwell,
> A little house, whose humble roof
> Is weather proof;
> Under the spars of which I lie
> Both soft, and dry.
> A little buttery, and therein
> A little bin,
> Which keeps my little loaf of bread
> Unchipt, unflead:
> Some little sticks of thorn and briar
> Make me a fire
> Close by whose living coal I sit,
> And glow like it.

Yet there is something else about that cottage home, something essentially countrified, sanctioned by custom. Not one of the windows or the door is open. They had plenty of fresh pure air without that; it came in at the back. Besides, no self-respecting country person used the front door, save for weddings and funerals. However, somewhere in the dim recesses of my memory I can recall that door being open and the sun pouring in on the coco-matting (pronounced 'cuckoo').

Now I have sufficient evidence to know that grandmother's garden was not always like the one shown in the picture. In fact it was not her garden at all, but grandfather's. He was a countryman, poor, thrifty and enterprising; but one could not get a long way on eight shillings a week, even in those days when you could get a farthing's worth of treacle at Broom's shop. So he grew seed and sold it, to help make those few more coppers. However, grandmother complained about this, because the "owd stuff" grew so high she couldn't see out of the windows, and thereby lost contact with anything that should pass by. She said, there was more in life than "scrabbin' arter wittals", and she liked a few flowers. I don't know that grandfather ever gave way, although he loved his Susannah dearly enough. But when the family became dispersed, and things were a bit easier, I suppose the garden reverted to flowers, and all was well.

I think grandmother must have been gathered into the old churchyard by the Backroad Hill when the picture facing page 49 was made, because as a little boy I remember the garden with little box borders. Now it seems to have been left to riot in petal and perfume. Mrs. Simkin has spread herself all over the place, but my word, how nice she do smell to be sure.

The pride of place has been taken by the old shrub rose that has climbed as high as the cottage ceiling. In all probability it is a China rose of a thousand petals, that has been cultivated and loved by every gardener for at least two years for every petal.

> Prick not your finger as you pluck it off,
> Lest, bleeding, you do paint the white rose red.

It could produce flowers from May to October, and its sublime breath seemed to fill the little space with a living loveliness.

> Then in that Parly all those powers
> Voted the rose the Queen of Flowers.

When my mother grew up to young womanhood, she, like all mothers in those days, suffered the loss of one of her little boys. It was a China rose that was planted on his, then lonely, little grave.

And was it not a white rose that the men of the Suffolks, plucked and wore after the Battle of Minden? The story goes that as the regiment was following up the retreating French they passed through a rose garden, and each man plucked a rose which he fastened to his head-dress. True to say, no one particular rose was worn by our men during the battle.

So then, on Minden Day (1st August), all battalions of the regiment wore roses in their caps, and in the event of a parade, the colours and drums were similarly decked in honour of that memorable victory. They were also worn on the Sovereign's birthday. As no special rose could be remembered as adorning that day, red and yellow roses were worn, those being the regimental colours. But those first Minden Roses must have brought back to the wearers, their garden homes of dear old Suffolk.

> Roses, the garden's pride,
> Are flowers for love and flowers for Kings,
> In courts desired and Weddings.

Then under the window of our garden is a fuchsia, pride of many a Suffolk heart; and in between, standing as thick as thick can be, are old-fashioned marguerites:

> To see this flow'r against the sonne spread
> When it upraiseth early by the morrow
> That blissful sight softeneth all my sorrow.

And somewhere is a bush of rosemary and a guerdon of lavender because "The floures of lavender do cure the beating of the harte," and "They are very leasing and delightful to the brain, which is much refreshed with their sweetness." It was always found in the garden of a country woman who made any pretensions to good housekeeping.

When the doctor came accompanied by his man, which was not often, he used to go to the front door. The more obvious approach would have been to pull in to the yard and go in at the back, which normally he would not have been averse to doing. But he so loved grandmother's garden that he preferred to walk down that little sanded path between the flowers.

He was of the old school, who bought a practice, bought a horse and a buggy and brooked no opposition. He used the bolus, pounded up his carbonate of ammonia himself and spread his own blisters. He wore the traditional broadcloth and took snuff. His man, who filled in his time looking after the surgery and the garden, used to hold the heads of those who came to have their teeth extracted. Sometimes they "whooly" screamed. Herrick knew him:

> When the artless doctor sees
> No one hope, but of his fees,
> And his skill runs on the lees;
>   Sweet Spirit, comfort me!
> When his potion and his pill,
> Has, or none, or little skill,
> Meet for nothing, but to kill;
>   Sweet Spirit, comfort me.

Sad to relate, the gulf between now and then is so vast, more than in years. Then one's mind was directed towards a romantic past, but now one is projected into an unknown future, a really horrid thought. The future seems to hold no opportunities for paladins in armour and knight errantry. That sort of thing is only reflected in the puppet theatres, whereas it was flesh and blood when grandfather tilled his fields and doffed his cap to the rector. I am glad to think, however, that, in some remote sunbeam ray, I can claim a relationship with that splendid heritage. For the memory is

As clear
As morning roses washed with dew.

12

GRANDMOTHER'S HANDS

——————————··✛··——————————

Berkshire char to her employer: "Those new people down the road are definitely not your class. That Mrs. Brown even scrubs her own floors."
"But you've seen me do that!"
"Yes, but Mrs. Brown knows how."

Two of the most revealing and expressive parts of the human frame that go to the making of a portrait are the face and hands. From what we can read of portraiture in general, both may be misleading. It was Max Beerbohm who complained that so few people looked like themselves; and apparently, the great portrait painters seldom painted the hands of their sitters. Reynolds, for example, drew the hands from those of his servants. When Millais painted the Glenfilas portrait of John Ruskin he suggested painting the hands from somebody else. Ruskin very truthfully remarked that his hands were unlike other peoples, and that it would be absurd attaching other folks fingers to his figure. And Burne Jones exclaimed of another artist, "Look at that hand. There isn't anybody else in the world can draw a hand like that." Amongst the varia spread out on Sir Winston Churchill's desk was his mother's hand moulded in copper. It was strangely akin to his own.

Evidently therefore hands are most expressive. Edward VI was trained how to hold his hands as well as how to enter a room with dignity and how to bow proudly. He was also schooled not to spit on the carpet, or to scratch his head with the forefinger of his right hand.

And, of course, there was the hand of the dilettante. "He had a **very** peculiar manner of always keeping his hands neatly

wrapped up in a napkin! There was something really touch-
ingly modest in the alacrity with which he returned them to the
wrapper the instant he had been disturbed and obliged to
expose them."

Leigh Hunt once wrote:

> I remember the impression made on me by a female plaster-
> cast hand, sold in the shops as a model. It was beautifully turned,
> though I thought it somewhat too plump and graceful. I fancied it
> to have belonged to some jovial beauty, a little too fat and festive,
> but laughing withal, and as full of good nature. I was told it was
> the hand of Madame Brinvilliers, the famous or infamous
> poisoner. . . . The woman went to the scaffold with as much
> indifference as she dispensed her poisons.

This brings me to my grandmother's hands and the question
of memory. I do not know how old I was when I first consciously
saw my grandmother, but I can see her now in my mind's eye,
although I rather think I never saw her again in this life. And it
is a curious fact that it was her hands that imprinted themselves
on my memory. Why? I cannot think, other than perhaps I
wondered how it was that elderly people seemed to have blue
blood rather than red in their veins. Perhaps it was the limp
way she held them and their long shape.

Of one thing I am very sure, her hands differed from those of
grandfather's, not only in sex, but in attitude. They had both
been brought up on the strong current aphorism, very true after
all, that "Satan finds some mischief still, for idle hands to do".
And therefore it was not often their hands were unoccupied.
Sometimes, in the evening, there might be a lull, although not
always on the distaff side, remembering:

> A man's work is from sun to sun
> But a woman's work is never done.

It was then perhaps you might notice the difference, because
when grandfather had nothing to do he didn't know what to do
with his hands, so they rested, palms upwards, and cupped on
his lap, as when his photograph was taken. Grandmother
usually found something to occupy hers, if it was only making a
red flannel petticoat and using a halfpenny to cut the scallops
to shape.

Of a truth, grandmother's hands belonged to the past, a long

unbroken past, delicate yet old, soft yet dexterous; and capable
and clever at doing the work of a housewife when labour was
tinged with pride. Hands that had been taught to bake and
brew, wash and sew, distil and preserve, weave and succour,
smooth and caress. It was by those same hands that she could
tell when the wort was at the right heat to add the hops, or
when the oven was ready for the bake. And they were hands
that sometimes, though seldom, could fold themselves up and
be at rest.

How grandmother came to be grandmother was something
like this. Grandfather was some bit older than her. She was but
a slip of a girl whom he had watched coming up, and when he
"axed" her the first time she said no!

> Poor honest John! It is plain he know'd
>   But liddle of live's range;
> Or he'd a know'd gals oft, at fust,
>   Have ways tarnation strange.

It is true one of his companions said to him the next day,
"Hullo, nabor, yow look kinder riled this marnin." But he per-
severed until she fared "toward like". When he finally "ringled"
her at his old parish church, he was all het up, making a noise
something like a bumble bee in a pitcher. The clergyman stood
there in his nice white surplice all cool and collected, and when
he said, all solemn like, "Wilt thou have this woman to thy
wedded wife?" grandfather up and answered right quick, "I
wool! I come hare a puppus!" And he never regretted his
impetuosity. Which was a sight better than the woman who
when asked—"Wilt thou have this man?" suddenly exploded
and said—"Noo! I 'oont", and marched out of the church,
leaving the parson and would-be groom staring at one another.

And so they set to work to make a home, and what a lovely
thing it was; at least the home I knew when I was so very small.
It was one of the Pugins who first saw that the art of the period
was a criterion of the quality and health of the society that produced it. If that was true, then the rot had not set in to that
Suffolk community, for it was an eighteenth-century art that
had blossomed but not fallen. You see, nothing became out-
moded in those peaceful years, so that what did for mother,
father and grandparents, did for the newly-wedded couple.

(*left*) 'The Old White Horse', Felixstowe. (*right*) The pumphead in a Felixstowe farmyard

A Felixstowe romance

Here follows a list of goods belonging to a Suffolk yeoman in 1681 and their then value, presumably for probate:

		s.	d.
For one peauter dish		1	0
,,	2 iron pottes	6	0
,,	a warming pan	1	6
,,	a hatchett		4
,,	a wooden can		3
,,	2 mealle poakes	1	0
,,	a Towe combe		4
,,	a paire of Andyrons and a peele	2	4
,,	a blankett and 2 bolsters	3	0
,,	2 chaires	1	0
,,	2 brasse skilletts	2	9
,,	a hooke		6
,,	a paire of sheetes	2	0
,,	a pashell and a bunching blocke		8
,,	4 old chaires	1	6
,,	daubing tooles	2	0
,,	a lether bottle		6
,,	an old bedstead	2	6

£1. 9. 2d.

From which you will notice that the two iron pots were of more value than the old bedstead.

Now the point is that, apart from the man's tools—he was evidently a plasterer or builder, hence the "Towe combe" and the "daubing tooles"—grandmother could have made use of them all and probably had some as old. Often enough a daughter inherited household gear from her mother, especially brewing utensils, and the old names for these things lingered on. For instance, her tubs were known as "becks", so these would include a hop beck, a copper beck and an underbeck or cooler. And a shallow tub would be a "keeler", which might also be used for washing day. She would have known how to brew almost by instinct, for she would have helped her mother, and the old terms would have been her common language, such as "gyle" for wort, "hilld" or "hills" for the lees or dregs, "lap" for small beer; and if the beer was turning sour it would be "mawbled".

8

She would have known something about cooking and making ends meet. Poor as they were there would be something in the pot, a pot very much like the two heading the list, even if it was only dumplings, which are alleged to have been the staple diet of those days. The old pot would have been hung over the fire by means of a "hake" or pothook; and there was always a fire burning summer and winter. The old dumplings were round, made of dough and yeast and boiled for twenty minutes. Light ones were called pot-cakes. To help these down a sauce was made of melted butter, vinegar and sugar. This was known as dip.

Pork and apple pie was a great favourite, placed in a dish in alternate layers until the dish was full. This was also associated with chitterlings and apple pie, each with a crust of dough. Pumpkin and apple pie was another, and pumpkin and raisins was yet another. All of which came with the apple season, and the first two with pig-killing, which certainly didn't happen every week, or month for that matter. There was a way in those days of keeping apples, as indeed everything else, including eggs. The latter would be kept in wooden hoops and moved slightly every day, so that the eggs rolled over, and thus prevented the yolks from sticking to the side of the shell. And sometimes they went in for a "pudding-pie-doll", which was their name for toad-in-the-hole.

But a "lamb-pie" was a sound drubbing, which she might have, or have not administered to her children if they had required it. Although I cannot think they did, so well were they brought up, three girls and a boy. And a lamb's leg is described thus by Moor in his *Vocabulary*:

"A nasal excrementitious particle—indescribable, except in the language of Spencer, as
        . . . draune bye foorefyngre foorthe
        From noose off schooleboye."

From all of this you can gather that grandmother's hands were always busy, for such was the way of poor folk. She had been brought up that way herself, even to find a moral in a needle and cotton when making her sampler, or passing-out piece in stitchery:

Seize the moments as they fly,
Know to live and learn to die.

Like Joan of Arc, who maintained at her trial that where her needle was concerned, she feared neither maid nor wife of Rouen. And although she was very poor, yet she was no "nip-cheese", or "a near split-farthing housewife". Moreover, although she was a Methodist, she followed the injunction given in the Church Catechism, viz. to keep her hands from picking and stealing and her tongue from evil speaking. Neither was she "scratch-pawed", or left handed.

When her children began to arrive, then it was that her hands were very full, because she brought them up by hand, as the saying is. And although she had only five, which was a mere hen's noseful in comparison with others at that time, yet she found them difficult to manage on a few shillings a week. However, she reared them right well, turning them into a credit to home and Suffolk. After all, she was no slut, like a sow and nine pigs in a rut, neither could the neighbours point a finger at her. They were similar to other children, and if they got the chance would eye the plum pudding wishly, and were really amenable to thick slices of buttered toast heaped up with brown sugar. Sometimes if they were extra dirty she would sing to them a little ditty:

> Wash the swine and make them clean,
>   To the mud again they'll jog;
> So some children I have seen,
>   Ever dirty like a hog.

But then she was full of those little catches, descriptive of folks in the village, little jingles which they never forgot—as for instance the one about women's colours. In those days, it must be recalled, they were as the good God made them, not as the hairdresser dyed them:

> Fair and foolish, little and loud,
> Long and lazy, black and proud;
> Fat and merry, lean and sad,
> Pale and peevish, red and bad.

And she had one about the fingers and thumb:

> Tom-thumbkin, Will-wilkin,
> Long-gracious, Betty-bodkin
> And Little-tit.

Unlike her neighbours, even her bucolic husband, grand-mother could write. True, the hand was a bit crabbed and the letter crossed and recrossed, but it was a real newsy letter that she wrote to her gals up there in wicked London, telling them of all sorts of little happenings that brought the old home to life. For instance, her "harren [hair] broom was wore up and the wooden pail had regular fallen to bits. But there, that on't last for ever, as the saying is." How Polly Vincent had just popped her head in to say that Ninny Free was taken comical again. "So I say to her, as how that 'ud be a funny world if there worn't comical people in it. Poor old Polly, she's as soft as a pound of soap, after a hard day's washing."

The letter would continue:

I'm a writing this by the light of a long-lady [a farthing candle], and that regular swale [waste] in the wind. But I must tell you Liza, I had one of them owd gipsies round here the other day. Her hands were as black as the stock [back of fireplace]. She wanted old clothes, but there, I hain't got none of them things as you know, so I cut her a great nobble off the loaf. And what do you think? She turned round and axed me if I'd any warmint that would eat it, for she wouldn't, and she hulled the whole lot on the old bumby.

I sent to Bessy's for some of her butter yesterday, your father like her's better than Rhoda's. But she had had a rare job with it on Tuesday when she churned, for that would keep on a blossom-ing [getting full of air].

Your cousin Maria have just been in. She say that uncle John have been taken queer again. They say he have got bloodless armenia [anaemia] but I don't hold with them new fangled com-plaints. Howsomever, he managed to eat a little sample for his breakfast.

But I must leave off now, and get ready to go up the wooden hill. Do you remember when you got your head stuck in a book, and I asked you how much longer you were a going to be? You used to say, "Wait you a minute, I have just got to Father Johnson, Nicholas Johnson's Son; or Son Johnson, Nicholas Johnson's Father." And that's where I be. Give my love to Ted, and the little old boy, bless his dear little head. Let's see, he'll be three when the tenacre is sown with wheat. How the time do fly to be sure.

Oh, afore I forget it. Young Kate has gone into service, some-where up your way. She came and see me just afore she start. Nice gal she is.

Then would follow the business of licking the stamp, sealing the envelope, addressing it, with her tongue hanging out and getting the finished bit of correspondence to Broom's shop. Grandfather could only look on as he was quite helpless in such matters. And so one more day would

Drop into the shadowy gulf of bygone things.

13

NAOMI LARTER

When I say that I know women, I mean I know that I don't know them. Every single woman that I ever knew is a puzzle to me, as, I have no doubt, she is to her self.

Thackeray

Naomi Larter had lived in Middleton all her life, first on the Moor Farm, when her father was bailiff there and when they kept geese on the Moor. Now the Moor Farm is on the turnpike that runs from Yoxford to Aldeburgh, and it was along that road that the news came of Nelson's death and his victory at Trafalgar. Her father could remember a brake, all covered over with evergreens and bunting, carrying the exciting information inland. And how folks ran off indoors fearing that Boney was following hard after.

She was a bright girl and might have answered the description given in the old ballad:

A country lass, brown as a berry,
Blithe of blee, in heart as merry,
Cheeks well fed, and sides well larded,
Every bone with fat flesh guarded.

Naomi loved the old home, its peace and security, and from the upper windows could just see the funny little spire of the church. Besides, on Sunday morning the sound of the bells, just a tingle tangle came across the fields in a most happy fashion. She never went to school, because they couldn't afford the penny a week, and the Church School was not yet. But somehow, by one means or another, she managed to learn to read and write her name. She was not very old before she was out to work.

Now the one great ambition for a respectable lass, or her
mother, was the Hall, and it was there that Naomi went as a
little kitchen maid. Her mother bought some calico from
Broom's shop and made her a regular new outfit, put her things
into a parcel, and they set off for Theberton Hall, one lovely
spring morning, in bright singing air.

Mrs. Doughty was a rather small person, but very much of a
lady, to whom the villagers were pleased to curtsey. They seemed
to think she was worth it. She was of a quiet sweet nature, and
her beautiful white hands hung loosely from the wrist as though
in want of employment, which was not really the case. She wore
attractive lace caps, and, regardless of the chilliness of the
Suffolk air, was never without a fan. This she used at all seasons,
creating a most unnecessary draught. She would sit well away
from the fire, with her feet on a little footstool, which was as
indispensable to her as the chair or sofa on which she sat.

Of course, little Naomi was taken on by the cook or housekeeper and seldom even caught sight of Mrs. Doughty; so far
removed was the one from the other. But she got to love the Hall,
a somewhat rambling house, with a garden full of flowers, peach
trees, and a big apple orchard. The old grey walls of the house
were festooned with roses and wistaria and the sweetest starry
jasmine, spangled over with butterflies and busy with humming
bees in the summer. To live in such a place, even below stairs,
was something of an education, although she had had no book
learning. And so Naomi grew up and became in time a housemaid and able to scratch her name on a bit of paper. It was not
long before Elijah Larter began to notice her (he thought she
was a real "Wenus"), and soon after that Naomi was married.
They found a home in a lovely spot along the Packway.

In her time Naomi had been a great traveller. She had pene-
trated as far as Wickham Market; which, as anyone knows, who
knows anything of the terrain about these parts, is a good twenty
miles distant from Middleton. More than that, she had spent as
much as a shilling on travel in foreign parts in her lifetime. That
was a lot of money when wages were not above twelve shillings
a week. She wouldn't have been so extravagant but for the fact
that she was placed in a fix. She had gone with her husband,
who was carter at the Packway Farm, when he went to the
maltings, and somehow or other lost him on the return journey,

so she had been obliged to come home by carrier. Further than
that it had meant two carriers at sixpence a time. Naturally
enough she was wholly put out, and so was Elijah for that
matter, particularly so as she didn't get back until late at night.
It was altogether a sorry business, but it provided her with a tale
of adventure for the rest of her life. When she got home all
Elijah said was,

> "Whatever aar yew bin a do'en?"
> "Been a do'en," I saay. "Aarn't I ha bin a lookin' fur yew?"
> "Waal, I towd yew tew waait fur me agin the chuuch."
> "Sew I did," I saay, "an' I might ha' bin thare still fur all yew
> ha' cared."
> "Now, thet bain't trew, Naomi, yew know thet bain't trew.
> Arter all yew are a growed women, an' yew knew right well,
> where we tewgether live. I kinder knew yew'd git hoom by hook
> or by crook An' sew yew hev. I hoop yew won't do thet agin."
> "Hoop I ont dew thet agin'," I saay. "Whatsomeever dew yew
> mean?" I saay, "Yew fare tew be whooly crazed."

Naturally enough she repeated this as often as she could find
anyone to listen. Some folks, of course, learnt it off by heart. In
fact she was gifted with a wonderful memory, and could even
enumerate the various articles that went to her first wash, sixty
or so years ago. They were so numerous that she fare got mud-
dled in the counting as she could only go up as far as ten.

She did not begin these confidences until she had sat back in
her chair, bolt upright, her hands firmly fixed on the arms, and
her feet settled on the floor.

Naomi lived to a green old age (so did her clothes), and having buried Elijah she became bedridden and rather lonely. Mr.
Hamilton used to go and read to her regularly once a week. She
set great store by these visits and, although she was hard of hearing, enjoyed them immensely. She liked the drawl of his voice.
One week Mr. Hamilton was called to London and completely
forgot his old friend in the rush to get away. When he came
home he remembered his failure and was full of apologies, and
she was equally full of lamentations. He managed to make peace,
but she became rather mysterious. There was a long pause,
broken presently by her creaky old voice.

"Well now, sir, I ha' gort suffen tew tell yew. Since yew wur
hare last, I ha' hed a wision!"

"Indeed," said the astonished rector. "What did that consist of? Do tell me."

"Well sir, I was a layin' hare, thinkin' like, as the saayin' is. Thet must ha' bin last Toosday, when yew wur away in that wicked Lunnon. By the way, did yew goo up in one o' them creepy, crawly owd trains? Thet mus ha' bin a little arter fower —lessways I think thass wat thaat wur. An' dew yew know, all on a sudden the door oped an' in come, who dew yew think, but my pore 'usband. He ha' bin dead this tharty year. But I knew ther wur him right enough.

"Well, sir, he come across the floor, quiet like, come up to my bed and strooked my hid twice, he did. Then he knelt down and said a bootiful prayer, and then he wanished. Now, sir, I can't help a-thinkin' thass a sign, thass a token, thet is!"

Mr. Hamilton listened attentively, then in the quiet voice he could adopt at times (otherwise he could "whooly" shout), he said, "Well, that was indeed wonderful, Naomi. I sometimes think these things are sent to warn us. What do you think that was a sign of?"

"Well, sir, I can't help thinkin' as I ha bin a layin' hare, but thet thass was a sign o' rain! A-coose, thet wur about the time thet thet owd Satan crossed the Crater!"

14

SMUGGLERS ALL

·····

Come, row the boat, row, to Levington Creek;
The boat full of roses as e'er it will stick.
Row the boat, row,
Yoho! yoho!

It is rather curious how smuggling has caught the popular imagination. It was a dangerous work, and danger always seems to court admiration. But at best it was law-breaking and a somewhat grimy business done on a dark night

When blood is nipt, and ways be foul.

It was also a trial of skill, and the result of considerable knowledge of times and seasons, untrodden paths, tides and places to land, inshore deeps and shallows and the vagaries of the sea. Then too, it was one way of adding a few shillings to a penurious existence, because the desperadoes who landed the stuff were not those who consumed it. They may have looked as though they had been fed on rum all their life, but that was most probably caused by exposure to the elements.

The romantic aura of the smuggler had hardly departed when, as a little boy, I visited my mother's home. Do you wonder that as I sat, probably on a home-made four-legged wooden stool, in one of those lovely old cottage rooms, I dreamt of Nelson and smugglers, poachers and ghosts. Yet I was scared beyond measure of the dark outside, lest I met the Dog Shuck or a bearded sailor with a peg leg, wearing a pigtail.

No less an authority than Southey has said that smuggling had its beginnings as soon as Custom-house duties were imposed. These started as early as the middle of the fifteenth century, when a law provided that all merchandise, whether entering or leaving this country, should be forfeited if landed or loaded in creeks or small landing-places rather than at the leading ports.

A reference to smuggling appears in the early *Minutes of the Wesleyan Conference* for 1744, of all places: "Extirpate smuggling, buying or selling uncustomed goods, out of every Society, particularly in Cornwall, and in all seaport towns. Let no person remain with us who will not totally abstain from every kind and degree of it."

It must have been very rife at St. Ives, for Wesley declares, "You will see my face no more."

The coast of Essex was said by an old native to have been "made a puppus for smugglers", and what went for Essex might have gone for Suffolk and Norfolk. It was at its height at the latter part of the eighteenth century and died a slow death in the nineteenth, coming to an end about 1856 when the coast-guards came into existence.

Nearly everybody was secretly in league with the smugglers, and the revenue officers often found themselves on dangerous ground. If one fell into the hands of these desperate men in a lonely spot, there was little hope for his life.

Scarcely any one of the maritime counties in those days was without its gang of smugglers, and many of our riverside and coastwise inns bear today the same name they bore when those gentlemen haunted their parlours. These inns thrived on the illicit trade in spirits and tobacco and in turn gave the smugglers every facility possible. Some were alleged to have even bribed the coastguards. Tradesmen were said to have had a hand in this dealing in smuggled goods. Many of the country gentlemen dabbled in this almost-romantic method of breaking the laws they were supposed to uphold, but which was generally excused as unjust taxation. One writer has gone so far as to say that the revenue man shot in some desperate affray was considered a tyrant who richly deserved his fate. On the other hand, the smuggler who perished whilst striving to place his kegs in safe hiding, was a martyr in a popular cause.

When England was at war with France, the presence of our ships in the Channel did much to discourage smuggling along the south coast. This led to a considerable increase in that traffic along the coast of East Anglia; which, after all, was always a most convenient spot for the landing of spirits smuggled over from Holland. The cargoes generally consisted of hollands, rum, brandy, silks, wine, tea and cinnamon. These things were greatly esteemed by the general public, particularly so if they could be obtained without the payment of Custom-house dues. Much in the same way as duty-free liquor is sought after by travellers today. Farmhouses and those big old country houses had their places of concealment for kegs and bales; and magistrates were not above sharing in the proceeds.

All along our Anglian coast the smugglers pursued their business. Any bit of lonely shore provided them with a venue, with a church tower to give them a bearing. The shore was lonely in those days, from Landguard Fort to Brancaster. The night would discern their ghostly figures and echo the muffled tread, perhaps respond in tremors to their feverish activities.

The *Ipswich Journal* is full of references to smuggling for the years 1729 to 1874, not all, however, connected with East Anglia. For example, in 1729 a terrible affray with smugglers was reported from Battle in Sussex.

The smugglers had landed vast quantities of Brandy and other Goods, and had got together above one hundred of them to carry them all off: of which the King's Officers having Intelligence, call'd the Soldiers to their assistance who were quartered in those parts for that purpose: these divided themselves into two parties and took two different routes, in case one should happen to miss them; and meeting at length with the smugglers received their fire first: then the King's party fired and killed three horses and shot one of the men through the leg. After they had fought a good while the smugglers fled and left one hundred anchors of brandy besides other goods and forty horses without doing any damage to the officers. [Anker: an English liquid measure for spirits, wine etc., containing about eight and a quarter imperial gallons.]

Then in 1735 comes this:

Yesterday morning five smugglers were brought up from Canterbury Jail in the Stage Coach guarded by a Cornet, a sergeant, a drum, and 13 private men belonging to Lord Mark Kerr's Regiment of Dragoons.

The smugglers were all men of substance, including a farmer, a grazier, a victualler, etc. . . . The same day a party of Gore and

Churchill's Dragoons guarded a cart loaded with 1300 weight of tea, to the excise office which they had seized at Botley Hill in Surrey, after a stout resistance in which one of the smugglers was killed.

A Suffolk affray appears on December 1735: "Last Sunday morning near Kesgrave in this County, was seized by Mr. Newby, Collector of Woodbridge, with the Assistants [sic] of the Dragoons, between two and three Hundred weight of Tea from the Smugglers with their horses."

The year 1736 records this under the heading of Ipswich: "On Thursday morning last, above five o'clock, a seizure of 600 weight of Tea was made by an Officer of the Customs of this Port, with the Assistance of some Dragoons, at Westerfield Green near this Town, when four of the Smugglers quitted their Horses and made their Escape."

Smuggling was carried on in earnest just now, as witnessed by the following: "On Monday last a Gang of about 20 Smugglers, well mounted and armed, were seen at Five o'Clock in the Evening about Low Layton, in Essex, with about 18 Horses laden with Goods, and making towards the Water-side."

Nothing to do with smuggling but too good to miss, is the following list of local casualties for October of that year: "Burnt 1, Drown 3, Excessive drinking 2, Murdered 1, Overlaid 1, Threw himself out of a window 1."

1743 gives us this: "Last Saturday Mr. Smith, a Custom-house Officer with some others, seized upwards of 400 Weight of Green Tea at West Ham, which was conveyed under a strong Guard to the Custom-house."

1744 reports that smuggling was carried on in a most gigantic style in Kent:

Sittingbourne, Kent, Dec. 20th., Last Week a Gang of 30 Smugglers broke open several Wool-houses belonging to Sir John Hale, Bart. and took from thence seven packs of Wool, they threatened to strip him of all he had, which is reputed to be worth £5,000. They ride about armed at Noon Day, and vow destruction to all who shall attempt to obstruct them; and the Numerous Robberies, Rapes and Insults that are committed make the People afraid to go about their Business. It is computed that upwards of 30,000 Weight of Tea, besides Brandy, etc, is run upon the Isles of Sheepey and Emly every year.

Yarmouth figures in 1744: "Yarmouth, April 19—On Saturday last one of the Officers of his Majesty's Customs in this port, seized at Caister, a village about two miles from hence, 2,200 Weight of Tea, and lodg'd it in the Custom House the next day."

A new way to deal with the situation is reported from Edinburgh:

Edinburgh, May 10. There are lately appeared in this Country a Zealous Spirit against Smuggling, which not only has affected those of a high Station, but spread also amongst the Farmers; an Instance of which happened this Week, when three of them seized a Smuggler and his Cargo, and carried him before a Justice of the Peace. Indeed it seems high time for Persons of all Ranks to bestir themselves, as in some Places the very Children learn to suck up the Brandy like Milk, a melancholy instance of which happened a few Weeks since at Kings Barns, where three Boys pierced a Cask of Spirits and drank to such excess, that two of them died the Day after.

Woodbridge reports for 17th October of that year: "A large capture of 3,000 gallons of Holland Geneva was made on board a vessel at Gravesend."

1764 brings us to Hollesley: "On Sunday the Custom House Smack took in Hollesley Bay a Smuggling Cutter, which had on board 213 Half-ankers of Brandy, Rum, Geneva, etc, a large Quantity of Tea, and other Goods, and brought her into this harbour [Harwich]."

This year also reports that the exportation of English sheep to France was prohibited; but by the following we see that the orders were eluded:

We are credibly informed that for several Months past scarce a Smuggling Cutter has gone over to France without carrying some English Sheep for the transportation of which they are paid a Bounty per Head. In a pasture near Roan [sic], in Normandy, there are near 200 for the Benefit of the great Woolen Manufactory carried on at that Place, and to keep up the Breed, the Climate of Normandy agreeing nearly with that of England.

It should be noted that sheep stealing was carried on at Walton Ferry by Felixstowe, it is said by maurading ships short of fresh meat. But it may well have been quite otherwise and in confirmation of the preceeding paragraph. It was so bad that farm labourers had to take it in turns after a hard day's work to do guard duty.

The river wall at Trimley, between Walton Ferry and Levington Creek, was regularly patrolled each night.

Week ending 22nd September 1764, the local news was comprised of the following: "On Friday a Smuggling Cutter was driven on Shore near Sizewell Gap, which the officers at Aldeburgh seized, together with 25 Halves of Brandy and Geneva, five hundred Weight of Tea, and between two and three hundred Weight of Coffee."

Week ending 13th October 1764: "On Monday a small Boat laden with forty-two half Anchors of Brandy and Geneva and a small Quantity of Tea was seized by the Commander of the Custom-house Smack belonging to Harwich. She is unrigged and laid up with two more lately taken by the said Officer."

This brings us to the Week ending 27th September 1783:

This week a woman was committed to Woodbridge Bridewell for giving false information of a large quantity of smuggled goods being concealed about 16 miles from that place. The soldiers were ordered to search for the goods and after they had been sometimes employed, were told it was only a scheme to amuse themselves.

"Monday last, was seized at Felixstowe, by Messrs Suter, superintendent of the Customs, and Fouracre, officer of Excise, 38 anchors of fine Cognac Brandy, 18 half anchors of foreign Geneva, and five bags of tea, which were conducted to the excise officer in this town."

Week ending 25th October gives us this: "Two waggons loaded with gin and tea were seized on Monday last from some smugglers at Happisburgh, Norfolk, and conveyed to the Custom House at Yarmouth. A party of light horse were sent from Norwich to assist the officers, the smugglers being so numerous."

As was previously stated, smuggling developed into a regular service. Small boats were used, but fast ships up to 200 tons burden were preferred. If a small vessel was surprised by some heavily-armed revenue cutter, the crew would "clap on Jackson", or, in other words, use every inch of 'muslin' to make good their escape.

One of these revenue cutters was the *Cynthia*, that ended its days off Southwold. I possess a coloured print of her with a marvellous sail spread. She was built by the famous Wanhill of Poole, where were launched some of the fastest smugglers and

privateers of those days. Indeed, she began life as a racer, and
the print shows her blowing up the Channel. It is of considerable
value.

It was said that gangs rode ashore fifty strong, and that farm
labourers were paid a daily retaining fee to hold themselves in
readiness and a golden guinea for the night of the run. In 1745
over 4,500 horse-loads were run in Suffolk in six months.

Preventive officers took all the risks of their dangerous job for
very little pay. There was no disability pension if they were
crippled in the service, and no compensation to their families if
they were killed. It is not surprising, therefore, if they found
means of recouping themselves in such circumstances. For
example, by law all captured vessels were supposed to be burned,
but often enough the officers would secure the cargo only. After
pocketing a handsome gratuity, they would look the other way
while the vessel escaped.

But just as the authorities connived with the smugglers, so,
when occasion required, the Government also was not above
using the runners for their own ends. Since these desperate men
were such excellent sailors and knew every creek and inlet of
their own coast, so they knew secret spots on the opposite coast
and were of great use to the Intelligence Service of those
days.

Smuggling at Aldeburgh was a regular feature; it must have
been an ideal spot. In 1720, so the tale runs, six vessels ran
cargoes in a single night. And, it is said, there were 300 men
along the shore to receive the goods. The Preventive officers
were useless against such numbers. If one considers the population along our coast at that time, however, the figures seem a
little exaggerated.

However, the tales still lack nothing in the telling. In 1778 an
armed gang ran a huge cargo in full light of day at Orford. Six
revenue officers were supposed to be present, but they were
powerless in the face of such large numbers assembled to run the
goods. They simply had to stand by and watch the stuff being
loaded on to the farm carts. In 1783 the tale was different. A
smuggling cutter drove ashore and the officers attacked. Beaten
off at first they called in the soldiers, and, after a clash of cutlas-
ses and handspikes, the cargo was captured. That was not the
end of the story. At dead of night the smugglers were supposed

Ploughing with Jolly and Ruby on what is now built-up land in
Felixstowe

Stackyard wall, mostly septaria, at Felixstowe

Brewers dray. A farmyard relic

Last stages of a fine old Suffolk wagon

to have broken open the revenue store and carried off the whole consignment.

Pin Mill apparently, was another venue for run goods; and why not? It was quiet enough, and the 'Butt and Oyster' must have looked on with beneficent hopefulness to replenish its cellars. (Incidentally, a butt was the Suffolk name for a flounder, not a stump of a tree.)

Churchyards were much in use on these occasions, and the parsons were blind to any activities of this nature. After all, what was wrong with a nice dry brick-lined grave as a hide? Who would want to look into such a place? It used to be said, in those times of long tenures, that many of these old rectories were famous for their brandy-punch. No one was likely to ask, when enjoying the brew, as to whether or no the ingredients had passed through Customs.

The year 1784 reveals smuggling as rampant, and we get this from the *Ipswich Journal*.

> Wholesale smuggling in tea and other contraband goods was the cause of many sharp encounters between the military and the smugglers, of which the following is an example:
>
> A few days since Messrs Stevens and Baker, Excise Officers, at Wadhurst, Hartfield, in the county of Canterbury, accompanied by a party of dragoons, fell in with a large body of smugglers, richly laden, at Eaton (Eden) Bridge, Kent, when a very sharp skirmish ensued, in which the dragoons were very busy with their broadswords. One smuggler had three of his fingers chopped clean off, and another, a very capital one in a way, received many cuts on the head, and several others being dangerously cut and wounded, they were at last obliged to yield, and leave the officers in possession of 19 bags of Hyson and Souchang tea, and six bales of muslins and cambric weighing each more than half a hundred weight, and valued, together at upwards of £1,000.

Another paragraph shows still more the gigantic nature of these illegal operations at this period.

> The capture of a smuggling vessel lately made by the *Orestes* was said to be valued at £30,000. We have since been informed that the goods taken are worth double that sum, several adventurers in this illicit trade have lost their all; one man lost £20,000, but he is supposed to be worth four times as much as the value of what was taken from him. There were on board 12,000 tubs of

spirits, and 18 tons of tea, but the most considerable was the bale of goods, consisting of fine lace.

An advertisement appeared offering one hundred guineas reward for the apprehension of a gang of smugglers who had nearly killed an Excise officer in Essex:

> Excise Office, London, 4 Feb. 1794.
> Whereas, on Sunday, the 23 of November last, about Four o'clock in the evening, Two men, supposed to be Irishmen, and to belong to a gang of smugglers, from whom a quantity of run goods had been that day seized, waylaid Thomas Bavin, of Herron Gate, near Brentwood, in Essex, and pursued him to a barn, from whence having dragged him by force, they beat him in the most inhuman manner, trampled upon various parts of his body, and Kicked out Four of his teeth.
> In order to bring the said offenders to justice, the Commissioners of Excise do hereby offer a reward of One Hundred Guineas to any persons who shall apprehend or discover either of the men concerned in beating the said Bavin, as before mentioned, to be paid by their secretary, on conviction of the party. J. Fisher, Sec.

A Chelmsford paragraph reports the following for the same year:

> The revenue officers of Burnham, lately returning with some seized goods, were assaulted by the crews of five free-trading cutters that lay in the river, and one of them was dangerously wounded. A few nights before, Mr. Francis, an active Custom House officer, master of the Bull at Hockley, was attacked, and nearly murdered, in his own house, by a gang of seven daring ruffians, the ringleader of which declared they came on purpose to destroy him; but after breaking two of his ribs, and giving him several violent contusions on the head, they were prevented from accomplishing their bloody design, by the providential arrival of some neighbours.

February 1784, brings us to Orford:

> On the 30th. ultimo, a seizure of 160 half ankers of gin etc. was made at Orford, being part of the cargo of a smuggling cutter that bulged near that place; upon which the smugglers rescued their goods, and in the scuffle two of the officers were much wounded. After the smugglers were gone, the officers made another seizure of goods out of the cutter, lodged them in a house in that town, and

sent to Saxmundham for a party of dragoons, but about twelve at night a gang of about 30 smugglers, all armed, broke into the house where the goods were lodged and carried them off in triumph.

Sunday last [May 1784] about two o'clock in the afternoon, a seizure of 57 half ankers of run spirits was made at Kettleburgh in this county, by Messrs Bell and Pope, supervisors, and Messrs Eugall, Mason and Spilling, excise-officers, with seven assistants. The same day, about four in the afternoon, as they were conveying these goods to Woodbridge, they were overtaken near Easton, by a gang of villains, about 30 in number (all apparently stripped to their shirts, except one), who with horrid imprecations, and expressions, of Murder! Murder! fell upon them in a most inhuman manner, with an intent to rescue the seizure; however, the officers made a noble stand, and a bloody engagement ensued, which lasted near an hour, when the officers put the smugglers to flight, pursued them several miles, and maintained the seizure. Almost all the smugglers were wounded, and many of them desperately, five or six of the officers' party were also slightly wounded. The officers and their assistants were armed with carbines, pistols, and broad-swords. It is supposed the noted George Cullum of Brandeston, was at the head of this banditti.

In Sussex there was daring combat with smugglers, in which the Custom officers were badly beaten:

Saturday morning, as a large body of smugglers were running a cargo of contraband goods, near Lancing Flats, they were fallen in with by the supervisor at Horsham, and a party of Walter's men, who seized 8 horses laden with tea, but had not got far with it on their way home when they were overtaken (it is supposed), by a party of the cutter's men, armed with blunderbusses, etc. who fired at the supervisor, but fortunately missed his body, though the contents of the piece went through his coat, and retook six of the horses. The supervisor lost his horse in the skirmish, had his men entirely dispersed, and was himself obliged to wade through a piece of water up to his neck to escape the further fury of the assailants; after which he got home safe and found that some of his men had arrived with two horses and 15 bags of tea. Two of Walter's men were missing, and it was feared that if the smugglers had not despatched them they had forced them on board their vessel, to be dealt with as the commander should think proper.

Another seizure of goods from smugglers was announced from Yarmouth in June 1784: "On Monday last was brought in here

by his Majesty's sloop *Speedy*, Jonas Rogers, Esq., commander, a
cutter laden with spirits, which he took at Thornham, he like-
wise chased and drove on shore at the same place a very large
lugger, which he sunk and destroyed."

In Parliament in 1784 mention was made of Bills relating to
Suffolk, and also a proclamation of outlawry against a batch of
notorious smugglers, one of which lived at Brandeston:

> Also proclamation for the surrender of Richard Hodskinson, of
> Worthing, Sussex, George Quartermain, of Godstone, Surrey, and
> George Cullum, of Brandeston, Suffolk, for aiding etc. in the
> rescue of tea, geneva etc. after seizure thereof by the officers of his
> Majesty's excise.

Another advertisement in relation to smuggling will tell its
own tale:

> Whereas I, Thomas Walker, of Wangford, in the county of
> Suffolk, Officer of Excise, did on the fifteenth day of April last,
> make a seizure of Eight Hundred Pounds of Tea, in the dwelling
> house of Robert Burgess, of Covehithe in the said county, a carpen-
> ter, as uncustomed goods. Now I make oath and say, that the said
> Robert Burgess was not in any sort or respect whatever, either
> directly or indirectly, concerned in giving information concerning
> the said goods being lodged in his house, either to me or to any
> other person to my knowledge, nor was he in any sort instrumental
> to such seizure.

Now follows the danger to which coastguards were subjected
in the prosecution of their duty:

> The *Hunter*, Yarmouth, revenue cutter, a few days since, dis-
> covered a lugger smuggler on the Norfolk Coast and put out Mr.
> Jay (second mate) and 12 people to pursue her; they were fired
> upon several times, notwithstanding which the officers came
> alongside of and attempted to board the smuggler, and the said
> Jay said, "Now, Mr. G.— I have caught you"; whereupon Mr.
> G. took up a blunderbus and shot him dead, and wounded
> another man, and loaded a canonade with an axe and other un-
> lawful combustibles, and discharged into the officer's boat, but it
> missed it and they got clear off without further damage.

In consequence of the great amount of smuggling and intoxica-
tion in the country, the Government had determined to place
some regulations upon the sale of spirits, which somewhat affected

the French, who for retaliation took off all the duties upon bran-
dies, which it was said places the English smuggler in a better
situation than he was before. For the duties remitted by the French
are more in proportion than what is taken from our rums and
British spirits. The brandy smuggled into this country was bought
on the Continent from 3s. to 4s. 6d. per gallon; at present this
article is selling at Dunkirk, Calais, and Boulogne from 1s. 6d. to
2s. 6d. so that the smuggler will have as much profit by the sale of
his brandy as formerly, and the spirit being in such high repute,
the consumption will be found not to decrease.

A terrible smuggling affray was reported from Norwich:

Saturday night, Messrs Green and Bennet, revenue-officers at
Snettisham assisted by a party of Elliot's light-horse made a seizure
of some goods landed from a cutter on Hunstanton beach, near
Lynn. A party of smugglers, headed by the captain of the cutter,
some of the crew, in attempting to rescue the goods, shot one of
the soldiers dead upon the spot; Mr. Green was killed by a musket
ball; Mr. Bennet was dangerously wounded in the thigh, and now
lies very ill. One of the soldier's horses was also killed in the
skirmish. William Kemball, the captain of the cutter, and Andrew
Gunton and Tho. Williams, were apprehended, and committed
to the castle on Tuesday last. As one of the above persons is admitted an evidence, it is hoped the remaining seven who escaped will
yet be taken.

A smuggling cutter was brought into Harwich having on board
a large quantity of spirits and 6,720 lb. of tea. It was intended in
future to burn these goods instead of selling them, as it was said
the smugglers were in the habit of re-buying them at a low rate.

In 1823 a foreign smuggling lugger was brought into Harwich
with a cargo of 116 half-ankers of foreign brandy, 109 half-ankers
of Geneva, and 29 small bales of tea. Six of the crew were British
subjects, and were ordered to be impressed into his Majesty's navy.

The capture of a Dutch smuggling cutter off the Whitby
coast is thus described in 1824:

Grimsby, Dec. 24. On the 16th., instant, the Revenue Cruiser
the Lapwing fell in with a Smuggling Cutter, about two miles from
Whitby at 4 o'clock a.m., when the Lapwing immediately gave
chase, hoisted her colours, and fired two unshotted muskets and
one six-pounder as a sign for the smuggler to bring to, which she
disregarded. A brisk fire was then commenced upon her for an

hour and a half, when she tacked and hoved to, with her head towards the cruiser. The firing then ceased. On passing within hail of the smuggler, she again made sail, steering W.N.W., when a second fire commenced upon her, she set her gaff topsail, and altered her course to N.W. by N. Finding the cruiser coming up she struck her sails, near Robin Hood's bay, after a chase of about two hours. The name of the smuggling cutter is the Dart of Flushing, with 13 men, laden with brandy, Geneva, tea, tobacco, cards, and Haarlem drops. The prize is estimated at £4,000 value. She is a fine sailing vessel, about 90 tons, rigging and stores new, and quite as large as the Lapwing. One man was wounded on board the smuggler by a musket shot. The prize was brought into the port of Grimsby, and the cargo secured in his Majesty's warehouse there.

Finally in 1784, we find this: "Monday last was carried into Yarmouth by his Majesty's sloop *Otter*, James Glassford, Esq., commander, a lugger called the *Peggy*, Butcher, master, laden with tea and spirits."

15

THE COUNTRY CHILD'S PEEP-SHOW

·•◦❖◦•··

There was an old woman had three cows,
Rosy and Colin and Dun.
Rosy and Colin were sold at the fair,
And Dun broke her heart in a fit of despair,
So there was an end of her three cows,
Rosy and Colin and Dun.

Long before Beatrix Potter created Peter Rabbit and Tabitha Twitchett, to say nothing of Jemima Puddleduck, the country child had found that world all ready made. He or she was on the most familiar terms with almost every living thing, because it bore the name of brother or sister. The only difference was that humans grew up to bear nicknames, which seemed to supersede their font names, while creeping, running and flying things remained in the common Christian class. How was this? Certainly the child itself couldn't have done it. Therefore it must have been an older child, one who never grew up, and whose mind was steeped in poetry.

This familiarity extended to ordinary domestic things, such as the kettle, which was a Betty; surely an apt name for something which sings so pleasantly to herald a cup of tea. An applejack was an apple turnover, a toothsome morsel when the crust had a bit of shortening in it and when it came out from the brick-oven all piping hot. But if it was a case of Boxing Harry, that meant going without food all day; which was not too good for Harry. In fact it was rather going Jack-at-a-Pinch. However, we must not omit Davy Dumpling:

> Davy Davy Dumpling,
>   Boil him in the pot;
> Sugar him and butter him,
>   And eat him while he's hot.

All little birds in East Anglia were called Dickey-birds, and they were very numerous. There was a Jack Snipe as well as a Jackdaw, the latter, of course, being a rare thief. Yet "The Jackdaw sat on the Cardinal's chair!" Then there was Tom-tit as well as a Betty-tit, and, of course, Robin Redbreast, who was always to appear on a Christmas Card when such things were first produced. Which brings to mind the pathetic little rhyme about:

> The north wind doth blow,
> And we shall have snow,
> And what will poor Robin do then?
>   Poor thing.
> He'll sit in a barn, and keep himself warm
> And hide his head, under his wing.
>   Poor thing.

As a companion piece came Jenny Wren:

> Robinets and Jenny Wrens
> Are God Almighty's cocks and hens.

In the process of time, so it was said, the two got married:

> 'Twas once upon a time
> When Jenny Wren was young,
> So daintily she danced,
> And so prettily she sung;
> Robin Redbreast lost his heart,
> For he was a gallant bird;
> So he doffed his hat to Jenny Wren,
> Requesting to be heard.

Jilly Hooter was the owl, but he was also known as Master William, whether the son of Old Father William I cannot say:

> You are old, Father William, the young man cried,
> The few locks that are left you are grey;
> You are hale, Father William, a hearty old man,
> Now tell me the reason, I pray.

Jack Bat flitted about at night and lived in the old church belfry with Master William, but made no noise:

> Twinkle, twinkle, little bat!
> How I wonder what you're at!
> Up above the world you fly,
> Like a tea tray in the sky.

Madge was the magpie, which you will remember Beatrix Potter turned into a doctor who was not above eating his patients' pies. I wonder he wasn't struck off the register for thieving. Which recalls the fact that it was that same author who wrote of a certain noble Lord: "He walks with his hands spread out, people say, to avoid picking his own pocket."

Charley was the wood pigeon, why so named I cannot say, unless it was because he was such a choosy eater:

> Charlie loves good ale and wine,
>   And Charlie loves good brandy,
> And Charlie loves a pretty girl
>   As sweet as sugar candy.
> I'll have none of your nasty beef,
>   Nor I'll have none of your barley,
> But I'll have some of your very best flour
>   To make a white cake for my Charlie.

If the pigeon's continual lament was something about being a poor boy, it wasn't because he would eat just anything. They had a rhyme about that:

> The dow (pigeon) she dew no sorrow know,
> Until she dew a benten go.

Bents, the coarse grass that grows by the sea-shore, remains uneaten by all save perhaps Jack, alias Neddy, Jenny or Betty Ass. Which brings to mind the little verse:

> Gee up, Neddy, to the fair,
> What shall I buy when I get there?
> A ha'penny apple, a penny pear,
> Gee-up Neddy, to the fair.

A starling was Jacob, a sparrow Phillip:

> For the soul of Phillip Sparrow,
> That was late slain at Carrow
> Among the Nunnies Black.
> For that sweet soul's sake
> And for all sparrows souls
> Set in our bead-rolls,
> *Pater noster qui*
> With an *Ave Mari*.

There were also Jack Curlew, King Harry the goldfinch, and Joe Ben the great titmouse; as also Jim Crow:

> Twist about, turn about,
> Jump Jim Crow;
> Every time I wheel about
> I do just so.

Young chickens were biddies and young ducks, diddles; a young cock was Roblet:

> *Cock:* Lock the dairy door,
>   Lock the dairy door!
> *Hen:* Chickle, chackle, chee,
>   I haven't got a key.

And a heron or a "harnser" was a Frank, which means free. Neither must we forget Mother Goose:

> Cackle, cackle, Mother Goose,
> Have you any feather loose?
> Truly have I, pretty fellow,
> Half enough to fill a pillow.
> Here are quills, take one or two,
> And down to make a bed for you.

Old Susan was a hare.

"Have some wine," the March Hare said in an encouraging tone.

Alice looked all round the table, but there was nothing on it but tea.

"I don't see any wine," she remarked.

"There isn't any," said the March Hare.

And Sukey was a breeding sow, which if she wouldn't eat her wittals they used to make a noise like "sus-sus" to encourage her. "Did you say pig, or fig?" said the Cat.

A frog was Jacob, but a Natter Jack was a species of toad to be found in the Broads' district, described as having short hind legs, prominent eyes, yellow lines along the back and black bands on the legs. His name may derive from the fact that he is sometimes known to talk or natter. Of the hedgehog they said:

> As I was going over Lincoln Bridge
> I met Mister Rusticap;
> Pins and needles in his back,
> A-going to Thorney fair.

And did you know they kept a tame hedgehog to keep down the crickets?

Nancy was a small lobster. Once upon a time you could have gone on the beach and asked a boatman, "Have you any lobsters?" He might have replied, "No, we've only Nancys."

> 'Tis the voice of the lobster; I heard him declare,
> "You have baked me too brown, I must sugar my hair."

Then, of course, there were great "owd" Jack pike, as big as "owd" sharks that infested the reedy dykes of the marshlands:

> How cheerfully he seems to grin,
> How neatly spreads his claws,
> And welcomes little fishes in
> With gently smiling jaws.

But Tom Poker was Puck, who lived in the chimney or in dark cupboards:

> For Tom the second reigns like Tom the first.

However, an earwig, alias an "arrawiggle", was also known as a Forkin-Robbin, because of its forked tail—surely a splendid appellation; while a louse was a nab-nanny. It can certainly nab, if it can't nanny, as old soldiers of the 1914–18 War can surely testify. And a snail was a hod-me-dod, which is hardly a girl's name:

> "Will you walk a little faster?" said a whiting to a snail,
> "There's a porpoise just behind us, and he's treading on my tail."

Father Long Legs we all know, but perhaps not everyone is aware that the flies that infest turnips were known as Jacks.

> And thick and fast they came at last,
> And more, and more, and more.

"Let's all move one place on." "Sap and sawdust," said the Gnat. But there appears to be no name for that "green little vaulter in the summer grass", the grasshopper.

> Whichever you please my little dears:
> You pays your money and you takes your choice.
> You pays your money and what you sees is
> A cow or a donkey just as you pleases.

16

BERNARD BARTON
THE WOODBRIDGE POET

························

His virtues walked the narrow road,
Nor made a pause nor left a void,
And sure the Eternal Master found
His single talent well employed.

Bernard Barton, the Woodbridge versifier and hymn writer
(1784–1849), never considered himself to be of any great
account, but had the immense good luck to find his friends
amongst those who were. Yet his genius was such that he is
being written about even to this day, for a book has just been
published through the University of Pennsylvania Press, entitled
The Literary Correspondence of Bernard Barton, edited by James E.
Barcus. That is more than will happen to some of our modern
poets who delight in the cacophony of words, or our artists who
deal in the abstract.

True, he was described by a writer in *Town Talk* as a "Small
poet of the Milk and Water School". "But", as he himself commented, "never mind, Milk and Water is not a bad drink in
warm weather; that is if both the items of which it is composed
are good of their kind."

Although he professed indifference to criticism his correspondence would suggest otherwise, for these letters show how
carefully he cultivated the friendship of poets, critics and editors
in the hope of getting favourable reviews. Moreover, the letters
tell of reviews and reviewers, the prejudices and popularities of
the time. He was a great lover of Cowper, Crabbe and Words-
worth, and corresponded with people like Southey, Lamb,
FitzGerald and James Hogg. His admiration for Crabbe led to a
friendship with the son, who, to Barton's great astonishment,

did not have on his shelves a copy of his own father's poems. Barton greatly enjoyed visits to an old lady at Mattishall in Norfolk, who remembered Cowper.

According to the *Suffolk Garland*, Barton was born in London, of Quaker parentage, but attended a Quaker school at Ipswich. He was apprenticed to a tradesman of Halstead, Essex, and afterwards married his daughter. He next went into partnership with a Mr. Jessup of Woodbridge in 1806 and set up as a corn and coal merchant. His wife died twelve months after the marriage, in giving birth to his only daughter, who, in turn, became a solace to her father until his death. Evidently the business did not prosper, for in 1810 he became a clerk in the bank of Alexander and Co. of Woodbridge, in whose employment he remained until his death.

It appears the Alexanders were Quakers also, and their business was widespread in the East Coast area. They figure in the melodrama of Maria Marten and the Red Barn Murder, because William Corder forged one of their cheques and made off with the money. The *Ipswich Journal* for the week ending 16th January 1864 has a notice of the death of a Mr. W. H. Alexander, a partner in the firm. It states:

> The deceased gentleman, who was a member of the Society of Friends, was a man of very unassuming manners, and was universally respected throughout the wide circle to whom he was known. He was a man of great energy, and throughout his life he had been not only an active man of business, but a constant and diligent scholar. His classical attainments were of a high order, and even beyond the ordinary range of Greek and Latin literature he had made such progress as is made by only a very small percentage of the men whose lives are entirely devoted to scholastic pursuits. In this town [Ipswich] Mr. Alexander was at one period of his life an active lecturer, and one of his lectures on Ancient Chronology was published. The town is also indebted to him for the supervision of the valuable collection of books and ancient manuscripts in the Public Library—the re-arrangement of which was not completed at the time of his death. Mr. Alexander was an Alderman of the Borough, Treasurer and Trustee to many public charities, and a member of the Ipswich Dock Commission. [But this in passing.]

Barton published many volumes of poems, but the title of one would aptly describe the whole: *Household Verses*. They did not win him a lofty niche in the Temple of Fame (I quote from the *Suffolk Garland*), but they made for him a home in many hearts. In 1846, Sir Robert Peel recommended the "Quaker Poet" to the Queen, as a fit subject for an annual pension of £100. However, Barton's finances were further supplemented by a collection made amongst the Quakers, of £1,200, originated by Joseph John Gurney. As he was always able to find time for his hobby, he celebrated his benefactor later in a poetical memorial.

Barton is best remembered through his friendship with Charles Lamb. At one time like so many other literary aspirants, he tired of his main source of livelihood and hoped to live by his writing. He therefore contemplated leaving the bank and embarking on the treacherous seas of literature. He wrote to Byron (of all people), who gave him sound advice. "Do not renounce writing, but never trust entirely to authorship. If you have any profession, retain it, it will be, like Prior's fellowship, a last and sure resource."

A reminder of this is recorded in the *Ipswich Journal* for 1864:

> An Ipswich paragraph records a sale of autographs and interest-ing letters, addressed to Bernard Barton, the Suffolk poet, by eminent men of all countries, and a letter of Lord Byron, advising him as to following authorship as a profession, and containing these lines:
>> You know what ills the author's life assail,
>> Toil, envy, want, the patron and the jail—
> was sold for £5.

Charles Lamb gave him equally good advice and his letters to Barton are amongst the most delightful he wrote:

> Throw yourself on the world without any rational plan of sup-port beyond what chance employ of booksellers would afford you! Throw yourself rather, my dear sir, from the steep Tarpeian rocks slap-dash, headlong upon iron spikes. If you have but five con-solatory minutes between the desk and the bed, make much of them, and live a century in them rather than turn slave to your booksellers. Keep to your bank and your bank will keep you. Trust not to the public: you may hang, starve, drown yourself for anything that worthy personage cares. . . . O the corroding, torturing, tormenting thoughts that disturb the brain of the

unlucky wight who must draw upon it for daily sustenance! Henceforth I retract all my fond complaints of mercantile employment; look upon them as lovers' quarrels, I was but half in earnest. Welcome dead timbers of a desk, that makes me live!

> Who first invented Work—and tied the free
> And holy-day rejoicing spirit down
> To the very-haunting importunity
> Of business, in the green fields, and the town—
> To plough—loom—anvil—spade—and, oh, most sad,
> To this dry drudgery of the desk's dead wood?

Apparently Barton complained that late hours and a sedentary life affected his health and gave him a headache. Southey advised him to keep good hours and never to write verses after supper. Lamb came up with some more of his characteristic advice.

> You are too apprehensive about your complaints. . . . Believe the general sense of the mercantile world, which holds that desks are not deadly. It is the mind good B.B. and not the limbs, that faint by long sittings. Think of the patience of tailors—think how long the Lord Chancellor sits—think of the brooding hen.

But it would appear that Barton was not above a bit of opportunism, for he had a most timely and propitious dream. He dreamt he was dining with Queen Victoria, who insisted on his writing something in her album out of hand. In this dreadful dilemma the muse put two stanzas in his head, which he never could have hammered out on his own. He most conveniently awoke with the verses intact in his mind and wrote them down as a sort of psychological curiosity. How very wonderful to be sure, the very thing that might tickle the fancy of Her eternal and immutable Majesty.

Some years later, the poet writing to a friend, said:

> Lord Northampton strongly urges me to print the dream verses. Though he gave them years ago to his friend Lord Monteagle, to present to the Queen, I should not wonder, if like me, he entertains doubts whether she ever really saw them. [Perhaps she was not amused]. At any rate he considers them quite a literary curiosity, and as such worth preserving, and wishes me with a suitable note, not going into all the details of the dream, *now* to

print them. They cannot, he says, be out of place in a book inscribed to the Queen; but the wording of a suitable note is a tick-
lish affair. It must not be done with levity, or familiarity, and it
would be as absurd to be over grave or solemn about a trifle.
Something bordering on the playful, mock heroic is the happy
medium, could one do it. Of course, neither he nor I dream wide
awake; but we agree in thinking it worth preserving as a curiosity,
and the object is to do this without taking improper liberties with
La petite Reine on the one hand, or compromising one's proper
self respect on the other.

As a Quaker he had no politics.

Politics of any sorts, or of all sorts, are not to my taste, but those
connected with electioneering tactics are the most loathsome. I
would as soon turn in three in a bed with two like Jemmy
Chambers [another contemporary Suffolk peasant poet] as to go
through the endurance of an election at Ipswich or Sudbury.
Believe me this is no *façon de parler*, for I should be truly sorry if a
dog of mine, for whose respectability I felt the least regard, should
be put in nomination for either places.

Barton certainly obtained a good deal of fame, for his poems
were said to be in every Suffolk homestead, and good little
maidens by the Deben liked to see a copy lying in their chairs,
beside their prayer books, before going to sleep. In 1822 there
was a party of English actors performing plays at Paris. One
evening, an actor of the name of Barton was announced, and
some of the audience immediately called out, inquiring if it was
the Quaker Poet.

Barton has a poem in memory of Robert Bloomfield, of which
I give the first verse:

> Thou shouldst not to the grave descend
> Unmourned, unhonour'd and unsung;
> Could harp of mine record thy end
> For thee that rude harp should be strung,
> And plaintive notes as ever rung
> Should all its simple strings employ,
> Lamenting unto old and young
> The bard who sung the Farmer's Boy.

Also, he must have been very fond of quiet, peaceful, rustic

Felixstowe. Presumably, like FitzGerald, he would have dropped down the Deben to land at the Ferry. He answered an enquiry for a beautiful spot in which to live, with the following:

Know'st thou the spot, on the verge of the ocean,
Which Flora hath blest, and mark'd for her own,
Where her votaries might fancy with fondest emotion,
The power whom they worshipp'd presided alone?

Know'st thou the beach, where the foam-crested billow
Bears no chilling blight to the shore which it laves;
Where the hue of the turf, fit for fairies' soft pillow
Is as fresh as the foliage which over it waves?

Know'st thou the spot, where each breeze that flies over
Like the bee o'er the flow'ret, must linger awhile,
For the woodbine and wild-briar woo the fond rover
To sip the rich perfume with frolicsome smile?

On that shore, where the waters of *Orwell* and *Deben*
Join the dark heaving ocean, that spot may be found:
A scene, which recalls the lost beauties of Eden,
And which fancy might hail as her own fairy ground.

And if it be true that when mortals are sleeping,
To leave their retreats the shy sea nymphs delight,
And while silvery moonlight their green locks is steeping
To sport on the confines of ocean through night:

O ne'er could the daughters of Neptune discover
A lovelier place for their revels than this,
'Tis a spot that might brighten the smile of a lover,
And which angels themselves might contemplate with bliss!

Enchanting Elysium! long, long may'st thou flourish,
To gladden the eye with thy verdure and flowers:
And may each future year which rolls, over thee nourish
Thine exquisite beauties with sunshine and showers.

And O may the taste, which hath plann'd and perfected
This fairy abode, its full recompense reap;
And, surrounded by sweets which itself hath collected,
Long enjoy the bright Eden that blooms by the deep.

This called forth a letter from Capel Lofft, the sponsor of Bloomfield:

We have read with pleasure your verses on Felixstowe, but with peculiar delight that calm, and soothing, and soul elevating poem, "The Valley of the Fern". I cannot but wish to know to what particular spot your muse attaches this pure spirit of immortality. I wish to give to this airy being a local habitation and a name—pure, touching, sublime—this is poetry.

(The spot was on the left of the high road leading to Melton from Woodbridge, behind what was known as Leak's Hill).

Barton's greatest friend was Edward FitzGerald, who thought highly of his work. Through a misguided idea that FitzGerald had offered marriage to his daughter, Lucy, a most disastrous contract was entered into, after Barton's death. Like John Wesley's, it was short-lived, and they parted, too set in their different ways ever to agree. In a posthumous edition of Barton's works, FitzGerald wrote:

The preparation of a book was amusement and excitement to one who had little enough of it in the ordinary course of daily life: treaties with publishers—arrangements of printing—correspondence with friends on the subject—and when the little volume was at last afloat, watching it for a while somewhat as a boy watches a paper boat committed to the sea.

A specimen of Barton's humour is to be seen in a letter he wrote to William Bodham Donne, of Bury, afterwards of the London Library.

I am going to be made a great Man! Not exactly called to the Peerage, but I am not sure the announcement of such an elevation being in prospect could have been more unlooked for. Four of my Townsfolk, or Neighbours, for two of 'em live out of Woodbridge, are building a new ship, and she is to be launched from the Stocks here this month or next under the name of *The Bernard Barton of Woodbridge*. . . . "Think of that, Master Ford"! If my bardship never gets me on the Muster Roll of Parnassus, it will into the Shipping List! If I fail of being chronicled among the Poets of Great Britain by some future Cibber, I shall at any rate be registered at Lloyds, along with the Spitfires, Amazans, Corsairs, and what not. The astounding fact was made known to me by one of the four owners a fortnight ago, and I have scarce recovered yet. I communicated it, too abruptly, to poor Edward FitzGerald, just as he was going to sit down to dinner with me, and he jumped up, chair and all, taking that and himself into the far corner of the room, professing that he could not presume to sit at the same table with one about to have a ship named after him. I wish I may bear such an unlooked-for honour with becoming meekness; if I do, I must thank my Quakerism for it, for it would ill befit one of our cloth to be uplifted in spirit by such an event.

The ship sailed eastward and was duly recorded in some far distant port as the *"Barney Burton"*.

His first volume of verses, *Metrical Effusions*, was followed by the *Convict's Appeal*, a protest against the severe criminal code of that time; *Poems by an Amateur*; *Napoleon*, dedicated to George IV; *Death of Shelly*; *A Widow's Tale* and *New Year's Eve*. After a long interval appeared *The Reliquary*, written jointly with his daughter Lucy.

Two of his hymns are in the new edition of the Anglican Hymn Book:

> Lamp of our feet, whereby we trace
> Our path when wont to stray;
> Stream from the fount of heavenly grace,
> Brook by the traveller's way.

And:

> Walk in the light: so shalt thou know
> That fellowship of love
> His Spirit only can bestow,
> Who reigns in love above.

These are set to quite nice tunes. Like Elizabethan lyrics, this sort of thing looks easy enough to produce; but if you have any aspirations that way, just try it. You will discover it needs a deal of metrical skill.

In one of his letters to Barton, FitzGerald thanks him for sending him a picture of dear old Bredfield, adding:

Some of the tall trees about it used to be visible at sea; but I think their topmost branches are decayed now. . . . From the road before the lawn, people used plainly to see the topmasts of the men of war lying in Hollesley Bay during the war. I like the idea of the old English house holding up its enquiring chimneys and weathercocks (there is a great physiognomy in weathercocks) towards the far-off sea, and the ships upon it. How well I remember when we used all to be in the Nursery, and from the windows see the hounds come across the lawn, my father and Mr. Jenny in their hunting-caps, etc, with their whips—all Daguerreotyped into the mind's eye now—and that is all.

And this is what FitzGerald said of Barton: "Few, high or low, but were glad to see him at his customary place in the bank, from which he smiled a kindly greeting, or came down with friendly open hand and some frank words of family inquiry—perhaps with the offer of a pinch from his never failing snuff-box."

The *Ipswich Journal* for 1824 has this:

A very pretty stanza by Bernard Barton, the Quaker poet of Woodbridge, upon the following quotation from a poem by Lord Byron, was given this week:
> "The Past is nothing! and—at last
> The future can but be the past!"

Is the *past* nothing?—think again!
  Whence then is *memory's* power
To ope the secret springs of pain,
  Or joy's delightful dower?
And is the future nothing too?
  Whence then the Hope and Fear
Which fill the Saints—The Sinner's view,
  When awful death draws near?

The sophist's specious lie abhor;
  And be these truths impress'd—
The Past must be accounted for!
  The Future—borne or bless'd.

He lies buried in the little graveyard of the Friends Meeting House in Turn Lane, Woodbridge, under a stone bearing the simple inscription:

Bernard Barton
died
19 of 2 mo. 1849
Aged 65.

His little house in Cumberland Street, now called Barton's Cottage, still stands; a peaceful study in weather-boarding and brick, with a Georgian frontage.

17

GRANDMOTHER'S LETTERS

··◦◦◦··

All letters, methinks, should be as free and easy as one's discourse, not studied as an oration, nor made up of hard words like a charm.
Dorothy Osborne (Lady Temple), 1627–1695.

My mother, like every other Victorian, was a great hoarder. This age of iconoclasm is the reverse (and perhaps it is as well), so that everything is torn down and destroyed. But hoarding has preserved so much that is delightful and revealing. Hence my grandmother's letters, not only to my mother but to her sisters, have been saved; since not even a postcard (halfpenny stamped) or a piece of string or a bit of paper that might come in for anything was thrown away in our old home.

Grandmother's letters are not the easiest things to decipher. Written and over-written on odd scraps of paper, more often than not on the back of a circular and by a steel pen, they take a bit of negotiating. The spelling is an adventure, and there is little or no punctuation, neither does the time factor enter into it, save on rare occasions. But they are so rewarding and revealing. We get such an intimate insight into the little details of country life in those now far-off days. I don't think grandfather was much of a hand at writing. He could sign his name, but reading between the lines, grandmother had to do his correspondence for him.

We see how cold the little house could be. How hard work it was to do the brewing and how it had to be done so frequently according to the weather. How absorbed grandfather was in his allotment. What she thought of her neighbours. How the chapel was nearly full and they always seemed to be having tea meetings and squabbles. What an orgy baking could be, and how they rejoiced when harvest was over and free from accidents. One thing, they reveal a very happy and devoted family; neither was there a whisper of the outside world.

I have just read the letters that passed between Queen Victoria and her brilliant daughter, the Crown Princess. There is nothing more revealing on both sides, uninhibited and artless correspondence, that is far truer to life than any biography. If that applies to royal lives, it is also conveyed in the simple trifles sent from a cottage home by a mother to her girls so far away. These old scraps, written with great effort, often by candlelight, bring back to life hands and hearts long dead. It was an unsophisticated age, conveying a message that was to last far beyond its years, sent under that most beneficent Act of modern times, the Penny Post, so that it becomes almost historic. Today, with telephones at a cheap rate(!), the words are dead as soon as uttered.

Be it recorded also, that both grandparents, separately, did make the tremendous journey to London, from dear old, quiet, rose-hung Darsham station, on the Great Eastern railway, to Liverpool Street. With what suppressed excitement they must have stood on the up-platform, watching the crossing gates being swung open, and the train coming round the bend in the distance, by Bramfield, in a plume of smoke. Would they survive the cimmerian darkness of the Ipswich tunnel and the long, dangerous journey? No wonder grandfather fell ill at the thought of it all.

The only complaint I can make is about the scraps of paper on which these bits of self-revelation were written; anything with a blank space was snatched into use, even to a note written on a folded sheet, such as this: "Walberswick, June 25, 1893. Please Sir, all being well I shall be at yours again on Monday Knight. E Sewell."

Now I happen to know that Mr. Sewell brought round an entire horse for breeding purposes, because once as a very little boy I was there when he arrived and took envious note that he had two eggs for tea. Neither was I allowed in the stackyard the next morning.

Grandmother immediately starts a letter under his signature and carries on with three clear sheets of notepaper, too good to miss:

Sewell ask for you every time he come or how my folks were.
You asked if we had any plums this year. No, about 6 on that tree
you got so many off 4 years ago. The other one can't expect it will,
as it was moved last year, nor yet bullaces, but rather more apples
on the old tree. I sold a peck and a half of black currants. Give the
postman 3 pints [currants, not beer], for bringing my medicine.
I expect I had drawing on for a bushel, with what I give away and
boiled down and made a bottle of wine.

Not long ago Mr. Aldridge came home with father one Friday
night and stopped perhaps half an hour and told father C.G. owe
them £5, and preaches the same. And that M—— by the school-
room owe him a lot for years, and they are both in the Class with
him. And don't you think it is gall to a man to meet with such.
Then he stalk up to the rostrum with his bass fiddle and seem as
they do. I told Aldridge I had been in the same fix with some professed people that seemed to be far more advanced, as if they
enjoyed religion so much more than ever I did.

I wish you were coming for the Harvest to be with me, but no
use. Thank God with all my fears I got over my brewing nicely
again. Put it in the coal house this time.

Now we move to "Dear Susie", her youngest and favourite
daughter, a letter written in October 1895:

I am now trying to write to you as I dare say you think it time I
should. Well, my dear, I don't forget you none the less. Well by
the day of the month we were packing you off last year, or will be
9th., the day before brother's birthday. Now it will soon be Ethel's
turn [a neighbour]. . . . I always seem busy, a lot of things to see
to this time of year. I made a little white currant wine, a gallon.
Well, just before father came up [to London] I looked at it,
thought I would taste if it was sweet and alright. Well, I set it in a
pot. Well, behold, as I pulled it out of the pot out came the wine,
the bottom was out of the bottle. Wasn't it a good thing I put it in
the pot, never have it served me so before. Well, I have brewed
once more. They are making us a new shed, not so big as the other,
not quite. Then father put the onions on granary, time he was
away, so I had to pick them over and measure them by the peck,
6 or 7 or 8 pecks altogether. So that took a time. Then the taters I
have had to help to get, so they are off the lotment. All done by
littles. . . . My eyes begin to be dimified, so must say good night.
Father is gone to settle up for the quarter day, expect him home.

It is "Dear Eliza" (her eldest daughter and my mother), who
receives this in 1892:

Yes it have been a wonderful time, sorrow and trouble seem to be every where, great men are took as well as the poorest. We see the death of Spurgeon a little in our paper. A great man but not too great nor too good for where he is. He have fought the fight and won the crown, haven't he? Well, I am thankful I am still alive, all of us.

Grandfather used to eke out his little money by growing seed. Here then is a reference to it: "We have mustered up a £ for the carrot seed, only one pound more. Maria's husband have sold nearly 5lb at Leiston for us, 2 shillings a pound. Good of him wasn't it?"

Here comes another, written as read, when a chapel tea gets mixed up with the brewing. Poor old grandmother.

Dear Girls, I thought I would brew as the weather was so nice, then it would be done for a time. So went and got my copper ready to fill to scald my vessels and things, they got so damp and mouldy. So I have to be so careful that the beer did not taste amiss. So father filled the copper and I set to and got it hot and scalt them all. They had no teachers' tea so are going to have a Society tea instead. So father was out every evening all last week. So the Thursday morning I got up and got the copper to boil. So I mashed and done it once more, thank God. I am so glad I had the strength given me to do it as it was rather cold. So that's got over if it comes cold for 2 months or perhaps 3. But I am very stiff from lifting, but I hope I shall soon get over that. So expect the tea will be on the 3rd. of March. So it will give you all time to get ready to come, but I shall be at home. I can't go, for when it is so cold it seems to go through me. So I keep at home. You will think I have put my letter together very funny to a young lady, but haven't seen so much of city life as you have. What I meant by father being out all the evenings, he's hardly ever at home, do he is off to bed a good time of the night. I could have had more of his help when I brewed, but no, on the lotment noon time and night, picking [?pricking] out more carrots for seed, so many each time. So have done them by going a little at a time while plenty have not done a stroke on either side. He helped me all he could but sometimes some one came so he could not come fast as I wanted him most last week. . . . I could send a bushel up.

Here follows a contretemps, written on the back of an appeal for Barnardo's Homes:

When the Bazaar was at Yoxford the Band from here was to have gone one evening with father. No one let father know nor no one seemed to know exactly. Father seemed to be nettled, then as I told him. Well he waited here till nearly seven o'clock, then he took his horn and said he would go as far as Joe Barham's. Well, Joe was then getting his horse ready to go. Button was at Rouse's corner, so two carts started, off they went. As they were playing at the Tun's yard, out come the man and wanted to know who was the master, so Godward said he was. "Who ordered you here?" He said he was master and ordered them off, so they all packed up and come home, so was home ½ past nine o'clock. I was rather amused at it although I did not say so to father.

I think they talk of having the S.S. Treat before harvest this year in July. Wonder if you will come here for your holiday then.

Dear Children. Just a word to say we are all getting on the best we can. We ought to have wrote before but you know what staying company is and no servant(!). [Grandmother had a very dry humour.] I wish Susie was going to stay longer as being harvest time father is not with them much. Is very tired bed time, from 4 or 5 mornings till 7 at night. If the weather is fine uncle and them will finish this week, not father as father go by the week and must do the stacks up, cover them. No accidents thank God, but it have been hot for them all and us as well, but not so hot for these few days nor yet nights. . . . I have felt so languid all the morning, now I know the meaning of it, the rain, but no thunder, not here, thank God. Have you thought of packing up to come for a month? Coming is all very well, but it is going away, then I think it is for the last time. Don't know if I shall bake as my flour is dark and old. Have had it for a long time, got a comb of wheat so had it ground. Had it in May or June, haven't much now. Father is down at house, thatching.
Can't rest much in this old place, so many fowls to see to, have to keep them from the rats. I think I have got over thirty chicks.

Dear Bec. Thank you so much and Susie for your good wishes for my birthday. I dare say you are looking forward to father's arrival in the City. Well, he have finished thatching, but not exactly finished as he goes by the week. The others have done, as they take it (the harvest), for so much. Hope father will finish up this week, all being well. We have got the onions off the lotment, harvesting them, so hope to get them under cover, and have got all the beet seed as well, so that wont take no harm till he come back. . . . I am sure your mistress is very kind to say what she did about making father comfortable. Well, you will have to get him another shirt like the one he come up with, as his other is not fit to bring up. Goodbye, dear Bec. Please tell the others about us. Am getting this ready for the butcher to post for me. Oh how hot, and the old flies keep buzzing on me.

Saturday after they left (visitors), I done my room up and swept the bedroom, laid the carrot seed on and done several other things, and Sunday morning it rained a little so did not go out till evening, went to chapel. Then Monday I washed a few (things) out, father went on Moor to thatch after dinner, so packed his fourses up. So had the afternoon to myself. Cut the onion seed off, soaked his shirt and one sheet, got the eggs up. Thank God father have done harvesting. Oh I am so glad so is he sometimes. So hot but no accidents. One stack in front the same as 4 years ago.

Here follows a bit of Victorian prudery, writing of her daughter-in-law.

Dear Liza, Hannah did not sleep here at all. I thought of last year when you were here. Did she tell you how she is again? Don't let the boy see this. [My brother, not me.]

Dear Bec. I feel as if I must thank you for your welcome letter. I did not worry much about coming up as I could not see how I could leave unless someone was at home, without feeling anything about Mary Godward. She would not be much use as she never have been used to going only her own way. But dear child, it seem too much now to leave father here alone, and myself I feel I am best at home, with many thanks to you both. But I am shut up here from one week to week and father is going somewhere nearly every night. I tell him he forget I am alone, and if I went to Chapel and left him at home alone I should not stop till them after meetings after the sermon. Then he get riled and say he can't give satisfaction at home nor abroad. So I say as little as possible. I know it would be 1,000 times worse if he was shacking about like some. But still I am alone.

The D's are still at that house by Buttons'. It was for debt for things he got to build them old houses to do them up. Now they are to be sold sometime this month. The youngest boy D. is married, so he claimed the pony and cart as his. Oh, what rogues they

are. Haven't we had beautiful fine weather sometimes? But have
been very dull nearly every other day last week, enough to make
one run away for a month. I am housed up, can't see into the road
who goes past, with the turnip seed. I tell father it is sickening to
have seed every year as he do grow it. Well, you don't know what
to get or to grow now a days.

Dear Bec. I thought I better say a few words to you about
father, he was very poorly 2 days this week, Monday, Tuesday.
Went to doctor's got medicine, so went to work Wednesday morning instead of Monday, so it put him back 2 days, so instead of
finishing Thursday night it will be tomorrow Saturday. So he
think if he come it will be tomorrow week to be there by Noon by
the first train Saturday morning. That's the time he have set. But
of course we will let you, some of you, or one of you, know when he
have asked Frank (the farmer), as he is not at home. . . . He was
bilious and the medicine done him good, but he will tell you
about it as I haven't time. We are all go, makes me dizzy nearly.
I want to go and cut the seed, some of it, then the onions lay in
backyard and we neither of us haven't much appetite, but thank
God I have been able to do as I have for him and myself. My feet
are as tender I don't hardly know how to hobble about for the
roads are so rough and dusty.

Dear R. I should have wrote before but who should come
yesterday afternoon but Aunt Ling. Perhaps she may come oftener
now she have started. I shew her your likeness. She say, "What's
that the mor [a Suffolk dialect word for mawther, a young girl]
Becca?" You know her homely way. . . . John Newson is going to
be married Thursday. Going to take the house and the mill. Today father had to go to Halesworth with the sheep wool.

I don't think Mrs. Foulsham will last long, if she is alive. Always
a nice respectable woman. Poor old man he will miss her, lived
together a long time, he bedridden. Well, the parting time must
come sooner or later. So you have some medicine for the nerves.
Yes, the money does go, but we must have things for it to keep us
going or the body would soon droop and wear out. Yes, I am glad
you haven't had cleaning to do. I can't clean yet I am always at it.
I get sick of it. I have a fire, I can't sit without one and can't sit in
the backhouse, old cold place. So it may go for what I care. Oh, I
am glad I am not forced to lay in bed. I can do as I like, a little
every day. What a mercy. Oh I hope none of us will have them
dreadful cancers. I don't think we shall, they must be dreadful. Old
Best is dead who lived at Middleton, old Tom Geater on the Moor.

So they keep going all over the world to their last home. Now dear, I must close, father is nicely well, everything is looking beautiful on lotment, very prosperous. So now with best thanks for all, I am, Old Mother.xxx.

Now father have done sitting up as it foaled yesterday Sunday, Oh what a night Saturday was, rained in torrents nearly all yesterday, Sunday.

There have been several auctions about. Several are going to move, but I am not this year, leave another year for a time as I don't know if I shall be spared. Thank God I feel better this time of year though I did nothing to boast of, but when I do feel better I know it and am thankful for it.

Mr. Woods came in a few nights ago and he said Jim Barham came to the station to meet Joe and he said he looked just what he is. He says his folks dare not be seen with such as him, so they don't correspond together. And he see Winter and he thought he looked not as he had seen him. He expect hard work to get along. Mary Godward told me Mary had a Mrs. Easter to nurse her that used to live at Peasenhall, James Smith's wife's mother. I expect she lives up there with them. She told me a lot. I won't talk it out, can't write it. Old Joe, by what C. G. said at Peasenhall, that Joe was drunk when he went, was really drunk at Peasenhall as they got home, so went there. I feel as though they are all given up to hardness of their hearts and that old drink will ruin them body and soul. Brother Charles' anniversary was yesterday. Dora was to say a piece. My what a contrast between Aunt Smith's children and ours. You was all brought up to work some sort and it never hurt you. Oh dear, I am sorry to hear about them. Joe is as bad as ever about drink. Well he can't conquer it, [the] craving for it, but I wonder what father would be like without it. But you see he don't have it only moderate.

"That's rather a sudden pull up, ain't it, Sammy?" inquired Mr. Weller.

"Not a bit on it," said Sam; "she'll vish it was more, and that's the great art o' letter writin'."

18

GRANDMOTHER'S VISION

························

"Yes, I have a pair of eyes," replied Sam, "and that's just it. If they wos a pair o' patent double million magnifyin' gas miscroscopes of hextra power p'raps I might be able to see through a flight o' stairs and a deal door; but bein' only eyes, you see my wision's limited."

Pickwick Papers

Rackford Farm backed on to the marshes, known colloquially as "maashes", and when grandfather tilled the fields and made excursions down the age-old drift, a sandy rutty track, everywhere was as quiet as a mouse. Indeed, it was so quiet that you could hear a dog barking as far away as the old smuggling inn, known as the 'Eel's Foot', a good three miles distant.

The farm stood, as it stands today, near the old Rectory Corner, and its meadows were divided from the Rackford Road by a ditch that seemed always full of meadow-sweet and forget-me-nots. The river that rose somewhere in Yoxford, flowed over the road, thus dividing the two parishes of Middleton and Westleton, and the horses and carts splashed through it, while the "owd hoss" always took a drink. Foot passengers went over a rickety, hollow-sounding wooden bridge on the rising side, and a little lower in mid-stream was a hole, known as "Mother Lumkin's", into which, it was said, a tumbrel and horse had disappeared, never to be seen again. Some folks thought it was an unwholesome place in which to live because of the fog and mists that often clothed the meadows that led to the sea. "Ugh!" they said, "we'd sooner live on the Moor, than that damp owd spot. Thet'll give yew the ague right quick!"

Now grandmother knew they were wrong, because that wasn't all fog; there were days when the sky was as blue as blue could be, and nights when the stars shone that bright you could see your way about in the open without even a horn lantern that gave out more smell than light. Often on a summer morning the sky was dappled with cirro-cumulus clouds tinted with an exquisite grey that presented the appearance of immense loftiness, while at evening the horizon seemed bounded by mountain heights. Then at harvest time there was the very unusual spectacle of the full moon rising out of the sea and the sun still going down over Middleton Moor.

As for the ague, neither she, nor John, nor her children, suffered from it, because they drank well-water instead of that which came out of the ditch. Grandfather in his wisdom used to say the people who suffered from ague lived near 'The Bell', because it not only made them shiver, but gave them a thirst as well.

Besides all that, there were little delicious bits to be met with in those marshes, not found elsewhere. Down at the end of the farmyard, by a gate that led directly on to the marshes, was a thick clump of elders. Here the song-thrush sang so finely that you might have mistaken its exquisite notes for those of Philomela herself. Then, farther into the middle distance, the coot clanked, the bittern boomed; while the sedge-bird, not content with its own sweet song, mocked the notes of all the other birds around. And, to fill in the scale, came the harsh melody of the reed sparrow.

And there were plants and flowers you couldn't find elsewhere, fairy rings, otherwise known as mushroom rings ("but then some fooks are ullus thinking about their innards"), marsh fern, bog pimpernel, sweet gale or bog myrtle and the marsh stichwort. Grandmother knew where they grew and showed them to her gals, to delight their adolescent country eyes and furnish them with abiding memories.

Sometimes grandmother would go and have a chat with Eely Joe, who lived in a crazy old craft moored to the bank in Rackford Run. After all, folks about there were of Saxon origin and liked eels as much as their ancestors. "Rum owd lot wur them Saxons."

That was not all, for on one occasion in the month of May, and once only, Grandmother saw a vision. She was so taken aback that she couldn't believe her own eyes. It happened like this.

She had gone to the pump for a pail of water, when she happened to look over towards Minsmere, when lo and behold she saw Middleton church (which was behind her), in the distance, not one but two churches, as there were in the olden times. . . Then, further over, the old city and port of Dunwich, that had "heerd" talk on and had slipped into the sea before even Elizabeth I was queen. There it was, as plain as a pike staff, just above the horizon, with little old boats (pronounced "boaats"), going in and out, no bigger than billyboy ketches. What did it mean? Church towers stood up and old gabled houses. She could see trees where she knew there were none, great "owd ellums", adding peculiar shapes to a ghostly scene. And she fancied she could hear a sound as though all the bells of the old city were ringing at once. Alas, as she watched, the scene vanished out of her sight and she felt lonely and scared.

When John came in for his dinner, which he did when he was working near at hand, she told him the story. It was his turn to look scared, for he kinder wondered if his Susannah was going out of her mind, or whether it was all a premonition.

"Whatever do you mean, gal? You must ha' bin dreamin'!"

"That I sartainly worn't," exclaimed the indignant grandmother. "I saw that as clear as I can see you and as sure as I'm a standin' here!"

"But yow ar'n't standin' yare a-sittin'," remarked her spouse.

"Well, then, sittin' thass all the same thing. Then all on a minute that wur gone. If I cud ha' called you, I'd a done so, but I felt regular spellbound. What dew yew think thet mean, partner?"

Grandfather thought for a minute or two, almost too scared to speak. Then a bright idea struck him. "Do you know gal, I kinder reckun thass a sign o' rain."

That was said merely to bolster up his courage and to allay the fears of Susannah. He knew what he was going to do, he was going to see the rector just as soon as he could. He felt sure he would be able to solve the problem. After all, Mr. Hamilton was a rare learned man, at least he ought to be with all those books in his study.

The Rev. Hamilton smiled, a kindly comforting smile. "I'm glad you have come, Mister Barham. Don't be alarmed, Susannah did see what she said she saw. I only wish I had seen it too. That was an illusion which sometimes happens in these parts and is known as a mirage. It don't mean a thing, except perhaps a change in the weather. So you can go home and bury all your fears in a good night's rest."

All the same, grandfather thought that was "a regular rum-un!"

19

YELLOW FLUTTERINGS

..⚜..

But oh, the very reason why
I clasp them, is because they die.

It is not often that the ordinary wayfaring man such as myself, has the extraordinary good fortune of blundering into a company of the immortals. But such befell me when I picked up for a shilling or so, a second-hand volume of local interest and on reaching home found it contained, interleaved in the text, a dozen or so autograph letters of more or less famous people at one time associated with East Anglia. It was a difficult matter to decipher the old writing, but the effort warmed the heart, if it tried the eyes. Little intimate touches of over a century ago, arrested from decay, all the more refreshing and exciting because they took upon themselves the nature of a discovery.

The first letter, complete with seal and cover, posted in Ebury Street, Pimlico, dated 1st March 1830, is from Allan Cunningham, "Honest Allan", and is addressed to Bernard Barton, Esq., Woodbridge, Suffolk. The letter, which is endorsed with the rounded, ingenuous signature of the quondam coal-and-corn merchant, bank clerk Quaker, evidently refers to Cunningham's *Lives of the most Eminent British Painters, Sculptors and Architects*.

37, Belgrave Place,
1 March, 1830.

My dear friend,
    Your kind letter with the manuscript of Lamb's came just in time for me on Saturday, the printer was clamorous. I slipt the letter into the narrative and with three or four songs of the poet

and painter and an additional anecdote or two the whole is in the press. I think the life will be considerably improved. Lamb made two mistakes—first it was Blair's Grave which was the folio or rather Royal quarto and contained the soul hovering over the body, and secondly the poems of Blake were published and printed though certainly little known. If more time had been mine I could have amended the life more than I have. I expect the new edition will be published immediately—but I cannot name the time—it depends of course on the bookseller. I shall *seek* and *find* some prints for your acceptance, but they run in setts of 20 and 30 and are difficult to get separate. Nor will you probably be much pleased with an examination of a solitary print or so—to put Blake right you should see the whole or a large portion of his works— they are so unlike other men's productions that they may startle in sample rather than delight. I shall be glad to see a notice of the book in Suffolk paper.

I remain in haste and affection,
Most faithfully yours,
Allan Cunningham.

It is a far cry from Lamb and Blake to Agnes Strickland, but not so far by the letters and the date. There is a characteristic epistle from that Suffolk authoress, addressed to the printer-publisher of the *Ipswich Express*. It might be mentioned, that the founder of that paper was a certain Mr. Sully, who, it is said, was the originator of the one-time popular amusement known as 'Penny Readings' on a large and successful scale.

If not counted much today, Agnes was a shining light in those days, now so far away and long ago. She was a great character. Her family had come over with Norman William, and that spirit flowed much in her veins. She was born at Reydon Hall, near Southwold, and from childhood was fond of verse-making and the writing of juvenile tales. Her great work was the *Lives of the Queens of England*, completed in twelve volumes in 1848. This was a joint work with her sister Elizabeth, who refused to be named on the title page. The young Queen Victoria accepted dedication of the work. Agnes was a partisan for the Stuarts and Mary Queen of Scots, who, of course, had a local reputation based on Framlingham.

Agnes could be met, driving in a pony trap in Southwold, with her sister, wearing her Georgian gold rings over her gloved hands! They were a gifted family, and the only one of her sisters who did not write married a printer, Robert Childs, of the famous family of Bungay printers. His brother, John, a great dissenter, came into prominence by refusing to pay the Church Rates and went to prison in consequence. It proved a death blow to those rates. Later the firm became part of Richard Clay and Son.

Agnes enjoyed a civil list pension later in life, and died unmarried. She is buried in Southwold churchyard with a younger sister, who was also her biographer.

Perhaps we might recall the little incident concerning her when she met the touchy, peculiar Borrow at a public function. She asked if she might send him a copy of her *Queens*, to receive the shattering reply—"For God's sake, don't, madam; I should not know where to put them or what to do with them." Then, turning to Donne, in a terribly loud aside, continued, "What a damned fool that woman is!" But was she? She evidently knew how to deal with the subject of her letter, who was later to become Bishop of Liverpool. But we will have the letter first and then something about the Rev. J. C. Ryle.

Sir,

In reply to your polite communication I hasten to thank you very cordially for sending me the "Express" containing your manly and sensible comments on the attack which the Rev[nd]- Ryle was pleased to make on me and the "Lives of the Queens of England", at the late protestant meeting at Ipswich. If the cause of protestantism received no more injury from my works, it would be matter of sincere congratulation to all true christians. But ignorance, bigotry and hatred of truth, which could prompt a protestant divine to recommend everyone to keep impartially written history out of the hands of women and children, are calculated to bring upon the reformed church an imputation, very mortifying to her sound members, as if her cause required to be bolstered up with falsehood, or that if certain facts were not concealed or prevented, women and children would cease to revere her and her doctrine. In this pitiful and degrading position does her professing protestant champion place her by his vituperations against an historian who has simply related facts, for which the fullest references are given, but I leave him to his own reflections on the duties injoined in the Law of God against false witnesses, if that does not convict him of having brought a railing accusation against me, nothing that I could say will.

I am very much beholden to your courtesy for offering me an opportunity for replying to the calumnies Mr. Ryle has thrown upon me and my work, but I am perfectly satisfied with what has been observed by you, sir, on the want of candour, to say nothing of the imbecility of bringing forward charges without evidence of the crime imputed to me.

My impression after all is, that the Rev. Ryle, has merely acted as the professional puffer of a very obscure talentless and bigoted periodical the *Churchman's Review*, and that on the same principle which invites parties particularly interested in spreading the sale of the commodity, to scrawl "Buy Martin's Jet Blacking" on the walls and houses of towns, where otherwise that article would remain unknown. I must therefore avoid the slightest approach to lending the aid of entering into a controversy, for the benefit of extending the circulation of that periodical, or, in fact, condescending to take any notice of the sagacious divine by whom the last number was so affectionately recommended to the attention of the protestant meeting.

I have the honour to be, with sincere appreciation of your courteous attention, and chivalrous defence for the honour of Suffolk, of a Suffolk historian, Sir,

Yours faithfully obliged,
Agnes Strickland.

Reydon Hall, Wangford.
P.S.

My letter is not intended for publication. I enclose an order on Mr. Cotman for the 9th. volume of the *Queens*, and should really feel grateful for the insertion of an extract from the preface of pages IX–X in the Express, because it will show the sources whence the new historical matter has been derived, which has excited such indignation from the liberal-minded Mr. Ryle.

The Rev. J. C. Ryle held two livings in Suffolk, one of which was at Stradbroke the interior of which he restored after the Victorian manner. He was also at one time, rector of Helmingham and this is what the Hon. Lionel Tollemache wrote of him:

His sermons were sometimes what might be praised as original or blamed as eccentric. I heard him preach on the downward course of an impenitent sinner. He described how the wretched man first thinks it too soon to repent, and afterwards thinks of it too late; and then he dies and Mr. Shavings is sent for to make his coffin. [Mr. Shavings was the pseudonym for a rich tenant carpenter, whose daughter had accepted the son of a very wealthy tenant farmer. It was wondered how this alliance would be acceptable to the farmer, this being in the days when prestige counted. When Mr. Shavings called on the farmer to know what fortune the bucolic grandee proposed to leave to his son, he was greeted with, "Not a sixpence. I find the blood, and you find the money". The marriage took place notwithstanding.]

It appeared that Mr. Shavings grew very red when his name was mentioned. It was said that when Helmingham Hall was, as it were, out of season, Ryle preached some remarkable sermons. One Sunday night in winter he exclaimed from the pulpit, "You say Cheer, boys, cheer, and There's a good time coming boys; but I tell you, There's a bad time coming, boys."

Educated at Eton he was a First-Classman, who argued that inspiration was nothing if not verbal. Tollemache goes on: "But though his theology belonged to the dark ages, both as parish priest and as a neighbour, Dr. Ryle was admirable. His sermons, though they may have been narrow and sometimes too colloquial, showed him to be what he was—a very able as well as a deeply religious man."

His tracts were very popular, not only in this country but in New York and in the Evangelical centres of the Engadine. He became the first bishop of Liverpool.

His third son, Arthur Johnston Ryle, lies in the churchyard of Old Felixstowe. He died on 20th March 1915 of spotted fever while working in the Y.M.C.A. hut at Felixstowe during the First World War.

Next we come to a letter of a latter-day Quakeress, whose handwriting was as lovely as herself. It is dated in characteristic Quaker manner: "II Mon. 2nd. 1833: Amelia Opie is rather impatient to receive the bread basket, and the other things which her friend Rix said should be sent & her ci-devant servant Hannah Davidson has promised to deliver this note. 70 St. Giles."

Amelia was a lover of bright colours, and one wonders if amongst the "other things" were some prisms: "Oh! the exquisite beauty of the prisms on my ceilings just now, it is a pleasure to exist only to look at it."

And here is a little picture of her by Caroline Fox: "She is enthusiastic about Father Matthew, reads Dickens voraciously, takes to Carlyle, but thinks his appearance rather against him—talks much and with great spirit of people, but never ill-naturedly."

Amelia Opie, née Alderson (1769–1853), married John Opie, the portrait painter, as his second wife. She was a successful novelist and poet. She became a Quaker under the influence of the Gurneys in 1825. There is a street named after her in Norwich.

This brings us by a natural process to the Martineaus and the famous Norwich Octagon, in this charmingly written letter addressed to "Thos. Martineau, Esq., Magdalen St. Norwich, 15–7–1822." The writer, of whom more anon, was an inveterate enemy of the old Ishmaelite, George Borrow, who pilloried him in the appendix to *Romany Rye* as the "Old Radical."

> My dear Sir,
> The bearer of this will be Mr. Radice of whom I have so often spoken to you. He goes to Norwich to make experiment of success. He is worthy of all your kindness and will I am sure be a very interesting acquisition to your society. I hope he will succeed in the object of his wishes during his exile. He is an enthusiast for liberty and his heart is not frozen by disappointment nor natural calamity. He is entitled to our best sympathies and I have no doubt will possess them—I mean yours—mine he has already.
> With kindest regards to Mrs. M., to H[arriet] (who will I hope be soon an Italian scholar) I am
> My dr. Sir,
> Yours most truly,
> J. Bowring.

Sir John Bowring (1792–1872), was a noted linguist, writer and traveller; he acquired many languages whilst in a mercantile house at Exeter. He was editor of the *Westminster Review* in 1824, and later appointed secretary to a commission for inspecting accounts of the United Kingdom. He assisted in forming the Anti-Corn Law League in 1838.

It is of great interest, in the light of modern developments, that he it was who obtained the issue of the florin as a first step towards the introduction of the decimal system of currency in England. His publications include accounts of his numerous missions, works connected with European and eastern poetry, hymns, and political and economical treatises.

There is also a letter from the distinguished James Martineau, brother of Harriet, directed to a would-be candidate for Manchester New College, a Mr. W. Jellie.

Manchester New College, University Hall, Gordon Sq. London, W.C., April 7, 1884.
Dear Sir:
Your application to the Committee of Manchester New College should have been addressed, not to me, but to the Secretary at Manchester. I have however forwarded it on your behalf to Mr. Dawson; who will lay it before the Comm^{ee} at its next meeting. The decision upon all applications is reserved for the meeting of Trustees which takes place after the Annual Examinations in the last week of June.

I remain,
Yours very truly,
James Martineau.

Of the Martineaus it might be mentioned, that Harriet was a successful author and a friend of Florence Nightingale, as also of Brougham and Macaulay. She visited the United States in 1834 and travelled in Egypt, Palestine and Sinai. She suffered greatly from ill health and successfully cured herself of one illness by hypnotism. She is described as being devoid of ambition or self-importance.

She was an apostle of freedom, equality in the social, legislative, administrative, religious and economic spheres; freedom for the American slaves, poor law reforms, land reforms which would improve the lot of the agricultural labourer, freedom for women to play their part in public life, freedom for them from humiliating and degrading regulations.

James Martineau (1805–1900), was a Unitarian divine, educated at Norwich Grammar School. He was the chief promoter and first secretary of the Irish Unitarian Christian Society in 1830. Principal of Manchester New College, 1869–85.

Next in order comes an epistle from Sir William Browne, a most worthy doctor of Lynn. It speaks for itself:

Hillington Hall,
Saturday.

Sir,
I this morning received your circular letter and so entirely approve of the new regulations you have adopted with the trades-

men at Harrow, that I shall be most happy in doing my best to have them carried into effect.

I shall write to my sons on the subject, and am

Sir,

Your humble servant,

To Rev. Dr. Longley

William Browne.

Sir William Browne was a Lynn doctor when the town was in great prosperity. Foote caricatured him in his farce, *The Devil on Two Sticks*. Before he died and was buried at Hillington, near Lynn, he directed that his Elzevir *Horace* should be buried with him.

Whilst on the subject of schools, there is a letter from Arthur T. Malkin, a son of Benjamin Heath Malkin, the learned headmaster of Bury Grammar School. In his day he was one of a literary coterie at the school, which included Edward Fitz-Gerald; W. B. Donne; the Romillys; J. M. Kemble, who became a fine Anglo-Saxon scholar; and James Spedding, editor of Bacon's *Works*. He was the author of *Pompeii*, *Historical Parallels*, etc.

In a letter from W. B. Donne to Fanny Kemble, sister of J.M., dated 12th October 1876, the writer refers to him: "A. T. Malkin is rejoicing in a good year for grouse, and signalised it by sending me a box containing five brace last month. Last year and the year before, he had but scarcely any, and shot only his rabbits."

Donne wrote an epitaph on the returned empty:

The Box
Herewith Returned
is
Sacred to the Memory
of
Ten Members of the Grouse Family
Who died September 1861.
They did Honour to Scotland and Good also to England
And before their Mortal bodies vanished
They Attained
The Odour of Sanctity.
The grateful receiver of their last morsel
By this Inscription
Records their Worth.

But to the letter:

Tuesday morning,
4, December, 1832.

My dear Sir,

I forgot to tell you how to dispose of the papers which you so kindly promised to look through. I go to Bury on Thursday; and shall remain till Tuesday probably. A parcel sent by the Bury coach will find me, addressed to Mrs. Hall's, Northgate Street.

A further error, was to leave the two portraits you gave me on a chair in your hall—I laid them down to put on my great coat, and forgot to take them up again. Do not estimate the value I set on them by my carelessness which is my besetting sin. One of Mrs. Leather's people will call for them to-day, or tomorrow. With best compliments to Mrs Turner and the young ladies, believe me—

Yours very truly,
A. T. Malkin.

And there is one, undated, from that pathetic, kindly figure, Samuel Laman Blanchard (1804–45). He was a clerk to a proctor in Doctors' Commons, and had been one, at 58 Lincoln's Inn Fields on the night of 2nd December 1844, to hear Dickens read *The Chimes*, the beginning of the public readings; and within a month or two he was dead. He appears in Maclise's picture of the group. When he started on his career of journalism, Lord Lytton warned him that "periodical writing is the grave of true genius". He edited George Cruickshank's *Omnibus* in 1842. His obituary notice pays tribute to his worth: "Beginning young and fighting an upward fight throughout—bravely, independently, without envy or uncharitableness." Surely, no mean tribute to any man, and so inherent in this letter:

Bedford Chambers,
Southampton St. W.C.,
Saturday.

You will have, my dear Cassia, to give your good friend Leonard, the genial welcome you purpose in the true hearty fashion that Alfred Place has so long adopted without my help, much as it is at the service of those who do the kindest things always in the kindest manner. I have but one evening that I can at all calculate upon as giving me a little leisure, and am not always sure even of that. Friday is the only night at any time that

I can at all set apart for a "look in" anywhere over a mile from the Strand, and I am even then, as I have just said, sometimes compelled to forego the little leisure and pleasure I had promised myself. This I know would be some days too late for the purpose contemplated, so pray tell Mrs. Maitland not to think "at all, at all" about me in this matter. I must trust to the accident of a chance collision somewhere sometime bringing Mr. Leonard and I together. Last evening I was hoping to slip away to Brompton to tell you all this much better and with more worth of personal apologetic explanation than I can now venture upon, but the soaking shower that caught me in Piccadilly necessitated my return. It is of course a disappointment to me but then I am getting somewhat inured to. If ever I get to sixty [he died at 45] I shall then expect to enjoy myself, but till then I have but little chance.

I silently commemorated the double anniversary of last Sunday but the sincerity of the wishes thought rather than uttered was as great as ever. Thanks for the Sp. Mag. which arrived safely.

In haste but with all the kindness of yore with the kindest regards you can convey for me to Mrs. Maitland

Believe me

Most sin-gularly the same,

S.L.B.

And here, as a tail-piece, is one from Sir William Parry, the Arctic Explorer, who was described by W. B. Donne as "the great hyperborean, Knight of the North Pole". It is a curious fact, but this type was always "Your humble", or "obedient servant"; but what if you trod on their toes?

Haslar Hospital,

Gosport,

22, June, 1847.

Madam,

Absence from home must be my apology for not before replying to your note of last Thursday; and I hope that my now acknowledging the receipt of it will be sufficient to answer the purpose you had in view.

I am, Madam, Yr obedt. Servant

W. Parry.

About ten years before the Donnes removed to Bury, their Mattishall house was occupied for a while by Sir William Parry, "the friend and crony of both 'the Bears'."

Sir William Edward Parry (1790–1855), rear admiral, commanded the expedition in search of the north-west passage, 1819–20, 1821–3 and 1824–5. He attempted to reach the North Pole from Spitzbergen by travelling with sledge-boats over the ice; but was finally stopped by the current which set the ice floes to the southwards almost as fast as the men could drag the sledges towards the north.

20

THE OLD WHITE HORSE

Whoe'er has travell'd life's dull round
Where'er his stages may have been,
May sigh to think he still has found
The warmest welcome at an inn.

I was greatly intrigued when reading the recently-published, *The Early Years of the Prince Consort*, to note that when the Prince set out from his home at Gotha to travel to England to meet his bride, the young Victoria, that the first stopping place was a small inn, known as the 'Last Shilling'.

I don't think we have anything quite as bad as that in Suffolk, but we have a large number of 'White Horses'. Why, I do not know, because a more fitting sign derived from our famous breed of Suffolk Punches, would be the 'Sorrel Horse', of which there appears to be only about three in the county.

Once again we find ourselves indebted to those old photographers, who made our past to live. They could not have forseen the sweeping changes that would come over our village scene; they were content to catch their moments etched in peace. And remember, the typical country inn picture facing page 112 must have been taken eighty or ninety years ago, for the present inn dates from 1904. Those were the days when Church Road was a muddy track, known as 'Hoss Lane', and High Road East was none other than the Walton Road.

It is a simple picture, taken with a time exposure, but it is full of romance. It must have been done early in the morning before anyone was about, for everywhere is as quiet as a mouse. Suffice it to say, it was a very old house, much older than the photograph would suggest, and that you went down steps into the interior of low-ceiled and oak-beamed rooms.

First of all, I wonder what became of that painted sign? Note the rather nice arched arm from which it hangs. Did some local artist limn the steed with its flowing tail? Alas, we shall never know, for it has gone with the wind.

Then note the dormer window, known in old Suffolk parlance, as a "lucum". In so doing you won't fail to observe the rather nice fire mark or plate, conspicuously displayed in the tiny gable. This is of great interest, because if my observations are correct, and I am sure they are, this was issued by the Royal Exchange Assurance Corporation, circa 1775. It is of lead and bears a view of the old Royal Exchange and a number. It may have been gilded but has been painted over. This would give some date to the façade as shown in the photograph.

Two quotations might be given regarding this. One dated 1684: "To prevent fraud in getting any policy after a house is burnt, no house is to be esteemed a secure house until the mark has been actually affixed thereto." In other words, it was the equivalent of a policy today.

It was this sort of thing that passed into a lampoon:

> For not e'en the Regent himself has endur'd
> (Though I've seen him with badges and orders all shine
> Till he look'd like a house that was over insured)
> A much heavier burden of glories than mine.

I wonder if that is in someone's private collection today?

The windows are fitted with the old wire blinds, so popular and unromantic, hang-overs of the Victorian cast-iron age. But the wooden shutters are a little more human and make it all cosy within when closed at night.

There is too, the old, iron footscraper at the door, tribute to a local blacksmith or foundry. It may have come from Garretts' of Leiston, but was a most useful detail to have about the place when dust was turned to mud. Do not fail also to note the stone step before the simple planked door. How many old feet, now lying in the nearby churchyard, stamped the clinging earth from off their boots before unsnecking the latch and going in. Those old bricklayers of local red bricks couldn't put in a tie-rod in a lowly building in those days without giving it a bit of twisty ornamentation. Perhaps the man who made it bore the name of Samuel, or that the missus' name was Sarah, or Susy. Who knows?

The painted sign over the door can just be deciphered with a magnifying glass. It reads:

George Moore
Licensed to Retail
British and Foreign Spirit
Wines Beer and Tobacco.

Now George was a bit of a character; he would allow no swearing on his premises, although it is said, he was not averse to letting himself go on other folks' premises. His wife was very religious and he respected her wishes and sensibilities.

Although George was not a shoemaker, his predecessor, George Hall, was, and that is his "owd" workshop at the side, with its half-hatch doors. That too was as old as old could be. The step here is much higher than at the inn door. It looks to me from the nature of its cutting, that it might have been a bit of the old church, or priory, or even Walton Hall itself. In fact it is just right for the job, for you can stand on it, lean your elbows on the bottom half of the door in comfort and watch George at work. You can tell him your rheumatics are right bad. His reply might be (if he hadn't run his awl into his thumb just at that minute), "Go you inside and ask the missus (who really kept the pub), for a tot o' rum." But he may have said no such thing, other than, "Go you home, partner, an' rub yare owd carcase with hoss ile."

If you study the roof of the inn carefully, I think you will agree it has been newly done, because the tiles look to me as though they are machine made. Those on the dormer are quite different, being the old shingle variety, the very same as on the old portion of the parish church. They might have been made at the brick kell at Alderton, across the Deben. The chimney suggests a spacious hearth, with possibly a flitch or two of bacon hung up to cure. You had to crouch well into the fire on a cold night, because the heat went up the chimney.

The size of this delightful old establishment would suggest that it was not designed for tippling. They couldn't have got many in at a time. Besides, the population wasn't all that large. No, you went in, had a pint (one penny), sat and talked about the crops, the recent tempest (storm), the stuff that was washed up at the Ferry, so you "heeard"; and then turned to enquire if old Missus Granny Newson still had her pint of beer served up in an old jug dead on the stroke of nine. It wasn't to be supposed she would have her finger nails cut now at her time of life. They were four inches long, but were useful in handling her clay pipe. "She's a regular owd rummun!"

But there is something else, not visible in the picture; the garden at the side, so well kept, full of old shrub roses and pansies and primulas, where the nightingales sang and the glow worms shone:

> Ye living lamps, by whose dear light
> The nightingale doth sit so late,
> And studying all the summer night,
> Her matchless song does meditate.

Remember too, this old inn of mediaeval origin was a centre for our society. Here would have been held the vestry meetings, and here the farmers and the local gentry would have stabled their horses while they attended the service at the parish church. Here the Volunteers were wont to muster and here came Mr. Gort, a name of some significance in those days, on horseback, to pay the "owd coproliters". Then too, the vet would, in all probability, attend here, his small and smart gig tethered in the yard. It was also a rendezvous for the local donkey boys with their charges, of which there were two packs; especially when it used to open at six o'clock in the morning and close at eleven o'clock at night. And from here, on festival days, they would have set off in horse-drawn waggonettes to fight the local giants of Kirton or Newbourne.

Here too you might have found the local rat-catcher, always a colourful figure in country life. And I'll tell you for why.

Periodically, there was a rat scare in Suffolk, particularly near the rivers and ports, sometimes raised because of the untimely death of rabbits and hares. Various causes for the increase of rats were put forward, such as the feeding of game in the coverts, the destruction by the gamekeepers of the vermin that preyed on rats. But it was pointed out the wet seasons were responsible for the death of the rabbits and hares, not plague as was feared. This is what someone who knew wrote on the subject:

It is generally conceded that the multipication of the rat in Suffolk began in earnest between 1884 and 1894, when agricultural land was pretty well unlettable, and was either kept in hand by the landlord or roughly cultivated by the tenant who in many cases paid no more than was sufficient to meet such outgoings as tithe and land tax. In those days ill weeds grew apace, the hedgerows thickened with them, and the bottoms of the woods became a tangle where the rats could romp at ease and liberty. They had plenty of fastnesses if attacked by the rat-catcher with his terrier, and even ferrets were not of much avail against them. They increased and grew fat. They were encouraged by the practice of building stacks in the open field rather than in the rickyard. These were the granaries where they drew their food supply.

And so we leave our old 'White Horse', remembering that, apart from a few cottages that formed the village round the church, all around were cornfields, east, north, west and seawards. While opposite was the Park, leading to the Long Dole and the Reed Pond, where lie the graves of Roman soldiers and long dead monks.

21

THE DEATH OF A FARM

························

Is my team ploughing
The one I used to drive?

One of the saddest things brought about by our overcrowded country is the death by consent of many of our farms. It is true that man does not live by bread alone, but neither does he by supermarkets. We are too apt to think we can live out of a tin or a refrigerator, but such is not the case. We live by the good earth and the produce thereof.

Agriculture is man's oldest industry, and farms are not something that spring up in the night. All of them in this country are of ancient origin, the care and development of many generations of hands. The Bible itself is a pastoral saga, beginning with a garden and the tillage of the soil. It is therefore not without significance that two words follow one another in my working dictionary. One is "Glean = to gather in handfuls after the reapers: to collect (what is thinly scattered)—to gather the corn left by a reaper—that which is gleaned: the act of gleaning." And the other is "Glebe = the land belonging to a parish church —Glebe-house, a manse."

Farming was a matter of living with heaven, though rooted in the earth, something of long, long tenure. By this occupation in depth a knowledge of the weather was gained, not to be obtained by scientific calculation. It was a case of weather wise, not otherwise. Little touches of nature told of coming events. All the speedwells, crocuses, pimpernels close up at a hint of rain, to protect their pollen. Fir cones close up for wet and open for fine weather. Birds fly low when it is fine but very high when a thunderstorm approaches. But if cobwebs are plentiful then it will be a fine day.

Old countrymen knew, as the one who said, "Well, I dunno, I'm sure; but as you axes me what's the day's going to do, I dun'er like the look on it—the clouds looks heavy some'our, the birds bain't singing, the flowers, especially the crocuses, be tight closed up and them blue-eyed weeds be gone to sleep. The cows be a-lying down. The cows lie down affore rain comes, to keep a dry spot for 'em selves, and the sheep do too. I see the bees all going into their hives and none coming out; they know more than we do."

It is difficult to believe, therefore, that the scene of the photograph facing page 128 is now a highway, duly paved and channelled in Felixstowe. It is John Perry ploughing with Jolly and Ruby in what was the Long Eleven Acre Field. This arable piece belonged to what was then known as Walton Road Farm, and John is naturally using a local-made Ransome's Y.L. plough. Strange to relate, not only has the scene completely changed, but the whole method of husbandry with it.

It is a peaceful picture, ploughing up the stubble, sea gulls in attendance, and not a house in sight. Bloomfield might have known it.

> With smiling brow the plowman cleaves his way,
> Draws his fresh parallels, and, wid'ning still,
> Treads slow the heavy dale, or climbs the hill:
> Strong on the wing his busy followers play,
> Where writhing earth-worms meet th' unwelcome day.

But it recalls the fact that ploughing, as with all other farm-worker's tasks, was an art; in this case, pulling a straight furrow, usually with a marker, such as a bit of a bush in front. A poor workman soon showed up his defects by leaving behind a crooked and badly-turned furrow. And remember, this form of animal-drawn ploughing was 2,000 years old. Oxen seemed to be before horses, and at Bocking, Essex, an acre a day could be ploughed with four oxen or two horses.

But Norfolk and Suffolk produced their own ploughs with two wheels, which could plough two acres a day with two horses. However, it was Mr. Robert Ransome, who came to Ipswich from Norwich in 1789, who produced and patented in 1803 a cast-iron plough share that would remain sharp in use and give greater economy over the then-existing steel share. He was the founder of the great firm we know today as Ransomes, Sims and Jefferies.

It is interesting to recall that in those early days of the business, on New Year's Eve, the workmen were supplied with bread, cheese and beer. With their employers they would sit round the embers of the last furnace lighted in the old year, telling old tales and singing old songs.

But to return to John Perry, who, like all countrymen, was very fond of flowers, his speciality being love-lies-bleeding. In the course of time he lost his wife and, like many another countryman, had to look after himself. When asked if he could make a custard, his response was a ready: "Yes, that's easy, eight eggs and a pint of milk." So he knew something of good living. Of course, they didn't always live like that. It was said the low standard of living of the Suffolk labourer brought about the rapid rise of the agricultural unions in the county.

The picture also suggests the forward look that was, and is, in every farmer's heart. Bloomfield wrote of it:

> In fancy sees his trembling oats up run,
> His tufted barley yellow with the sun;
> Sees clouds propitious shed their timely store,
> And all his harvests gather'd round his door.

Felixstowe farmers were blessed by having the best bread-producing land in the kingdom, and also in having the famous coprolite pits ready to hand. The discovery of this natural fertilizer was made accidentally by a Levington farmer as long ago as 1718. These petrified nodules had to be washed and then ground before being mixed with sulphuric acid before being of any use. They must have added greatly to that great climax of all farming, the Harvest Home. It is interesting to note that it was in our Colneis Hundred there was a special form of request made by the harvesters if working too fast. Someone would call out—"Blowings, my Lord!" which was allowed them.

An old Suffolk farmyard is full of interest, and when it comes to a breaking up it is a sad story. The old barns decay and crumble bit by bit, the outhouses begin to shed their protective walls. But one or two cows still bellow through an open door-

way, and hens poke about into any place that affords an opportunity. In the old days the milkmaids took the pail to the cow,
but now the cow is marched to the milking shed. These old
animals were as individual as their owners, and many are the
tales they evoke.

There was the case of the new arrival, who was anxious to
find her way about. Nothing loath, she climbed up the stairs in
the old barn, a narrow steep ascent of some thirteen ladder-like
wooden steps, to the corn loft above. She weighed fourteen stone
if she weighed an ounce, and how she got up that staircase was
a marvel. Having got up, the great problem was how to get her
down without injury or broken leg. They lined the stairs with
straw, wrapped her round with straw also, and as by a miracle
she slid down on her rump without so much as a scratch, or
leaving a dent in the stairs.

In the case of the farm I have in mind, at one time the cows
would be led to and from their pasturage by an old donkey, who
knew his way about. But the cows knew what to do, as when they
took themselves home before time, marching into the farmyard,
having broken down the bit of barbed wire that kept them in.
When soldiers came to man this bit of coast, it was found the
cows were dry, much to the cowman's surprise. They had been
milked by the cooks, so the troops had sergeant-major's tea for
once.

In the farmyard of which I write were two wagons. One, now
destroyed, was a brewer's cart made by the Bristol Wagon and
Carriage Works. It had stood for many a long year unused, but
took a mighty long time to die. It was built for double shafts,
and the hubs were as clean and well-greased as when it trundled
along the roads. Its elm timbers were as firm as when it left the
maker's yard, while the iron work would have done justice to a
battleship.

My next is a magnificent specimen of the wheelwright's art,
and I believe hails from Helmingham. The farmer's name is
still on the nameplate. What it must have looked like in all its
painted glory I can only imagine, but enough remains to show
of a great creation. Its decorated front has gone, but the tooling
on the ends of the summers (the longitudinal timbers of the
floor), and the bolsters, show what pride had gone into its con-
struction. Here again, it is a double-shafted wagon. There is a

possibility that this old relic will be preserved, with those splendid wheels that ran so smoothly and easily when it went to market and was taken for granted. George Sturt would have been pleased to own this, the perfect combination twixt wheelwright and blacksmith.

There used to be five stacks in the stackyard after harvest, now, of course, there is not one, and fodder and bedding has to be bought in to maintain what is left. This is not an economic proposition. How good those stacks looked, well built to a pattern and size, shaped to allow the rain to drip off, and yet to stand up without prop or stay. The thrashing was done by an old steam engine which would be quite an attraction today if seen in action.

This brings to mind the tale used by a local preacher who saw to his dismay that his congregation was going to sleep. He woke them up good and proper by announcing that "Brother Ally made the stack bottom too large for the size of the stack cover." Their ears soon responded to that bit of folly.

And there was the story about the stack that was heating up. The farmer decided he was going to open it up, but was told, if he did, it would burst into flames. He sent his son along to the local brigade to warn them there would be a fire in two hours time, so they could get ready. He got out his stack-tester, a steel rod in two halves, that could be screwed together to make one six feet in length, thrust it into the stack to find that it was true enough. The fire took place, and the firemen arrived with their old horse-drawn engine, having been given the longest notice they had ever received.

Alas, alas, stacks no longer take on the old and beautiful pattern, and the hay needle is no longer required to ease out the truss from the stacks, cut by the hay knife. Neither is the pony plough required, otherwise known as the small farmer's implement. Before this was thrown on the dump, it could be pulled by a pony or even a donkey and did a good job of work.

But the farm must have been of some consequence, for where else would you find a pump head to match the wonderful specimen in the picture facing page 112. I wonder if it came from some old priory when that was broken up. The escallop shell, leaf spray and stars would almost suggest an ecclesiastical origin. And remember too it is a silent link with a water supply that served our fathers since civilization began. That long link has only been broken in recent years by piped water and water boards.

But what shall we say of the magnificent old wall that surrounded the stackyard? It is of fortress strength, built mostly of septaria, gleaned from our beaches, mixed with free stone that came out from ruined castles and priory walls. It has a brick coping, now thatched with climbing plants and was built for all time rather than a day. Tennyson would have found much to ponder over if he had seen such a token of stability.

> Flower in the crannied wall,
> I pluck you out of the crannies,
> I hold you here, root and all, in my hand,
> Little flower—but if I could understand
> What you are, root and all, and all in all,
> I should know what God and man is.

Going to market meant Ipswich, which took four-and-a-half hours, leaving at 6.30 in the morning, and arriving at the 'Sorrel Horse' about eleven. There would be as many as fifty horses in that yard. They would bring back a ton of meal. The carter would get his horses ready over night, the harness and the horses shining with polish and pride. One of these old fellows thought nothing of swallowing eight pints before breakfast (not milk or water).

On the return journey the horses hot and sweating from their exertions, would stop for a drink outside the Walton Hall farm, where there were ponds each side of the road. If the carter was not careful, they would lie down in the water, harness and all, and sink in the mud, in an effort to cool themselves.

One other small matter, but of great significance. Before sanitation came to our township, the retreat was placed at the further corner of the walled garden. A visit on a dark, cold, rainy night must have been of necessity indeed.

22

A FELIXSTOWE ROMANCE

On 29th March 1921, was laid to rest in old Felixstowe church-yard, one John Scammell, formerly of the Royal Navy. He had joined the Navy in 1853 at the age of 21, just in time to be present at the Siege of Sebastopol. He was then serving in the old wooden walls of St. Jean d'Acre. During his twenty years service, his ships included the *Meander* (1856), *Blenheim* (1858), *James Watt* (1859), *Royal Adelaide and Pembroke* (1862), and the *Penelope* (1869–73).

In 1873 he transferred from the navy to the coastguards, in which service he continued until 1887, when he was discharged with the rank of chief boatman. During the whole of that period he was stationed at Woodbridge Haven and continued to live at Felixstowe until his death. His medals included the Crimean for 1854 and 1855, one Buller Medal for the same dates, the Long Service and the Good Conduct Medals.

His remains were interred with semi-naval honours, the coffin being covered with the Union Jack, upon which were laid his cap and tunic, with his medals. A party of bluejackets from Shotley Barracks, under a C.P.O. acted as bearers. The only mourners were the members of his family. After the committal by the Rev. Walter Horne, two naval buglers sounded the 'Last Post'.

I wonder how many Felixstowe veterans were entitled to wear that Crimean medal, with its pale-blue ribbon, edged with gold, and its oak-leaf clasps? It bears the head of the youthful Queen Victoria on one side, with the date 1854; and a warrior being crowned by a wreath, borne by the angel of Peace, and the word Crimea on the reverse. John Scammell may well be the only one in our parish churchyard.

Sebastopol was one of the many blunders in that wretchedly mismanaged campaign. Together with Balaclava it was a Russian naval port on the Black Sea, and one of the veiled objects of the war was to destroy Sebastopol and thus end Russian naval power. The British Army was riddled with cholera, had little or no transport, was landed in an unknown country without any previous reconnaissance. But hopes were high and it was thought that the taking of Sebastopol would be a walkover. However, the siege was to last eleven weary months. Sebastopol could have been taken almost immediately after the battle of the Alma, attacking it on that side, but delays and indecision proved fatal. A line of battleships was sunk across the entrance to the harbour, thus blocking an entrance to the Allied Fleet. Now came a clash of opinions. Sir George Cathcart, commander of the British 4th Division, was for an assault. He said he could walk into Sebastopol almost without the loss of a man, but Lord Raglan would have none of it, and decided on a siege. On 29th September naval Commanders were directed to disembark the siege guns, and the army began to sit down before the fort.

The bombardment began on 17th October, but was a failure. Our ships were of wood, while the fortress was of stone walls six feet thick. However, the cannonade managed to destroy the principal Russian fortifications, and every enemy gun was silenced. The Russian commander thought it was all over and that we should walk in, but, with our usual inexplicable mismanagement, we did not. The consequence was that the Russians were able to make good their loss in time to prevent this.

Our army before Sebastopol caused Lord Raglan great anxiety. So many were sick that the others had to do double duty. On 18th June an assault was made by raw British troops, and failed. Lord Raglan's heart was broken, and a few days later he died. Peace was not signed until April 1856.

However, after Crimea, came a great change for the better. Staff colleges were set up; conditions in military affairs were completely altered; commissions, promotions, medical and hospital services, supply, clothing and cooking were all improved. And the name of Florence Nightingale became a household word.

And so our hero came home, and, whilst still in Her Majesty's

Navy, sent a Valentine card from Woodbridge, on 13th February 1863 in an embossed envelope, with a penny red perforated stamp to a Miss S. Hall, Vernon Villa, Felixstowe, Suffolk; and thereby hangs a tale.

Sophia Hall, who responded to the appeal made on that day, was a housemaid at Vernon Villa, with the Login family. (This is now Ridley House, Felixstowe College.) The Logins could only have newly arrived in Felixstowe, as Sir John died there that same year. The Halls, at the other end of the social scale were an old Felixstowe family, and their graves line up in the old portion of the parish churchyard, dating well back into the eighteenth century. It must be remembered too, those were the days of marked social distinctions and Sophy would have curtsied in no uncertain manner when she passed such as Mrs Allenby (mother of the Field Marshal), another great dame of the period who lived nearby, when she passed her in the byways of the village. She expected and received that sort of deference.

The Valentine itself is a beautiful example of cut-paper work, and is really three-dimensional, a worthy token from a sailor of the old navy. Cupid asleep in the shells lies amongst real seaweed, coloured green, silver and red, and there are real shells; while the inset nautical picture of an old three-masted frigate is veiled with tinted gauze. The lacy floral border is comprised of orange blossom:

> Accept my dear this Orange Flower,
> The pride of love's delicious bower.
> It is the Flower for Bride's to wear,
> When plighted vows are proved sincere.
> Place these sweet flowers on Hymen's shrine
> My own beloved, my Valentine.

Three stars shine in the gauzy heaven, although it is still day. Another cupid holds aloft a sign, "Forget me not", while on the opposite side a silver dove carries a sealed message of peace.

No wonder Sophia Hall treasured this token of a good man's affection. If it cost but a penny to post, thanks to Sir Rowland Hill's great and beneficent measure, the token itself cost fourteen pence to buy, which price is still clearly marked on the back. And that was a lot of money in those days. But how proud the young sailor must have been when he found it in a stationer's shop in Woodbridge, the very thing he was looking for. (I wonder if he found it at Mrs. Matilda Jemima Catchpole's, Bookseller and fancy repository, Thoroughfare?) One can almost sense his delight as he bought the stamp, wrote the address in his best penmanship and posted it.

I wonder how it was delivered at Vernon Villa, and if it arrived on the day, because Felixstowe's first postman, John Bloomfield, was not appointed until 1875. However, the 'Fludyer Arms' acted as a post office, and the mail driver might have spotted it, entered into the romance and run along to that old seaside villa, with, "Here you be, Sophy, there's suffen for ye!"

This old relic of Victorian days is now held in the proud possession of Sophia's grand-daughter.

GHOSTS

The shadows fall: must ghosts to darkness keep
In some strange half-lit isle of moon-blue space?
Must they live on, and wail and groan and weep
O'er might-have-beens, tomorrows void of grace?

With visage bloodless, hands with malice blent,
Their restless souls seek rest in unwashed stains.
Some cruel deed lives on, its toll not spent,
Lurking in deathly chambers, gripped in chains.

These are the ghosts that yester-year may claim—
But not of mine and me when shadows fall;
They hold a ghostly progress, flame on flame,
While mine keep tryst serene, without a pall.

Old faded faces, kind, with hearts as kind;
Old hands that worked the flail and brewed the beer:
That baked the bread, and brought old ways to mind,
Old country fancies, fraught with homely cheer.

They lived in peace, in peace they came to die
(Their tenor told the years their life had told),
As side by side they came at last to lie:
Their fields, corn-laden, all their tale could hold.

In clasped album still their shades are found;
And as we turn the leaves they bid us hail
In rising voice; lisping old words that sound
Softly anew, as in a twilight tale.